ESSENTIAL LIBRARY OF SOCIAL CHANGE

DISABILITY RIGHTS MOVEMENT

IHSS
KEEPS ME
INDEPENDENT
A CALIFORNIA BUDGET
R THE 99%
California
Family Recovery

ESSENTIAL LIBRARY OF SOCIAL CHANGE

DISABILITY RIGHTS MOVEMENT

by Tim McNeese

Content Consultant

William N. Myhill
Director of Legal Research and Writing
Burton Blatt Institute, Syracuse University

CREDITS

Published by ABDO Publishing Company, PO Box 398166, Minneapolis, MN 55439.

Printed in the United States of America,
North Mankato, Minnesota
052013
092013

THIS BOOK CONTAINS AT LEAST 10% RECYCLED MATERIALS.

Editor: Melissa York
Series Designer: Emily Love

Photo credits: Rich Peroncelli/AP Images, cover, 2; Evans/Three Lions/Getty Images, 6, 55; Bettmann/Corbis/AP Images, 8, 41, 47, 66, 78; Mark J. Terrill/AP Images, 12; North Wind Picture Archives, 14, 21; Stock Montage/Getty Images, 18; Jerry Cooke/Time & Life Pictures/Getty Images, 25, 56; Library of Congress, 26, 29; Lewis W. Hine/Library of Congress, 33; Interim Archives/Getty Images, 35; Jacques Boyer/Roger Viollet/Getty Images, 36; C. F. Chambers/Library of Congress, 38; Sonnee Gottlieb/Hulton Archive/Getty Images, 48; Donn Brinn/AP Images, 51; Marty Lederhandler, File/AP Images, 62; OR/AP Images, 65; AP Images, 68; Sal Veder/AP Images, 73; Lana Harris/AP Images, 75; Dennis Cook/AP Images, 76; John Prieto/The Denver Post/Getty Images, 81; Jeff Markowitz/AP Images, 85; Melanie Stengel/Bettmann/Corbis/AP Images, 86; Barry Thumma/AP Images, 89; iStockphoto/Thinkstock, 92; Mel Evans/AP Images, 97; Red Line Editorial, 100, 101

Library of Congress Control Number: 2013932965

Cataloging-in-Publication Data

McNeese, Tim.
Disability rights movement / Tim McNeese.
p. cm. -- (Essential library of social change)
Includes bibliographical references and index.
ISBN 978-1-61783-886-6
1. People with disabilities--Civil rights--Juvenile literature. 2. Discrimination against people with disabilities--Legal status, laws, etc.--United States--Juvenile literature. I. Title.
342--dc23

2013932965

CONTENTS

CHAPTER 1

OVERCOMING DISABILITY

Twenty-year-old Robert L. Burgdorf Jr. was ready for work and could not have been more proud. The year was 1968, and young Bob was home from college for the summer. He hoped to soon be walking in his father's footsteps. Robert Sr. was a longtime electrician and a member of a union in Evansville, Indiana. That summer, the union was sponsoring a special program allowing young men to work as apprentices with their

« **Before the 1970s, people with disabilities were frequently segregated in the workforce.**

fathers or other professional electricians. Young Bob was prepared for his first day on the job as a summer student assistant. He suited up in his father's typical work uniform: jeans and a T-shirt, a hard hat, and an electrician's belt bristling with tools, "slung low over my hip like a holster."[1] He certainly looked the part of an electrician. In fact, he reminded himself of his father.

Robert Burgdorf Sr. had helped prepare his oldest son for this special day. He had familiarized his son with the tools of his trade. And now father and son could work together. Excited about his first day on the job, young Bob "felt adult and manly."[2]

But that first day, and all it represented for the son of an Evansville electrician, would soon turn to disappointment. As the sons gathered at the local union hall with their fathers, the foreman soon spotted young Bob. He immediately took him aside and told him he would not be needed. With a matter-of-fact tone, he said words that cut the young man to the heart: "We're not hiring any cripples here."[3]

For nearly 20 years, Bob Burgdorf Jr. had lived with a physical challenge. When he was only months old, he contracted childhood polio. The disease left his right arm paralyzed. At the time, there was no cure for the disease. His parents recalled how their milkman, who delivered

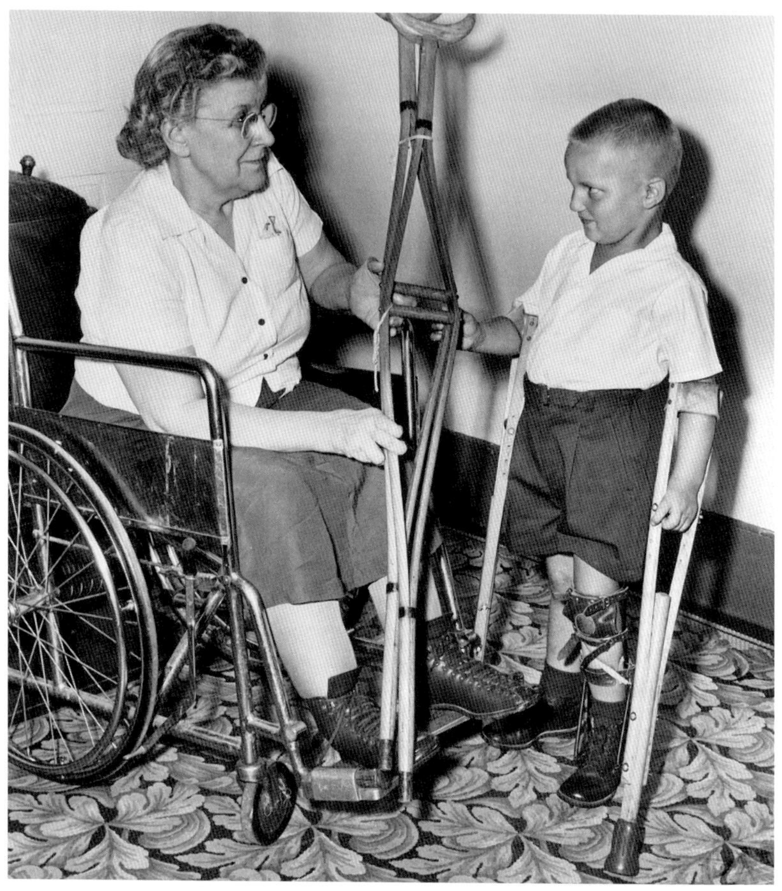

Many polio survivors required crutches, leg braces, or wheelchairs.

milk to their door, stopped coming to their house for fear of getting the disease.

Yet the elder Burgdorf had not allowed his son to use his condition as an excuse. He had drilled into young Bob the belief he could do anything he put his mind to. His son had taken the lessons to heart, learning to do things with his left hand, including playing basketball. His nonfunctioning right arm had not kept the young man from doing almost anything he wanted. But now he was being denied a dream—to learn the trade of his father.

Young Bob later described how he had wanted to shout at the union foreman: "You can't do that. It's against the law."[4] But, in 1968, there were few antidiscrimination laws in the United States. Little protected people like him from being denied opportunities in the workplace. Angry, he could only return home. Once there, he bitterly removed his tool belt and hat. "My macho bubble was burst," he later recalled.[5]

POLIO: A PLAGUE OF THE YOUNG

Polio also goes by other names, including infantile paralysis and poliomyelitis. The condition is caused by a virus that attacks the central nervous system. Polio arrived in the United States by the late 1800s, though it was not initially widespread. In 1916, however, there was an epidemic with 27,000 cases leading to 6,000 deaths.[6] The disease seemed particularly cruel as it often targeted young people, usually between the ages of five and nine. Dr. Jonas Salk developed a polio vaccine in 1954, which helped eradicate the disease in the United States within a few years.

Frustrated and angry on that disappointing summer day in 1968, Bob Burgdorf Jr. could not see what would happen 20 years later. He went on to graduate from

LIMITED MOBILITY: PEOPLE WITH DISABILITIES STAYED HOME

During the 1980s and before, many Americans with disabilities faced rejection from society. A 1986 Lou Harris Poll reported that 17 percent of people with disabilities had not eaten at a restaurant during the previous year. This compared to 5 percent of people without disabilities. One out of eight people with disabilities never went to a grocery store, compared to one out of 50 among people without disabilities. Two-thirds of people with disabilities had not gone to see a movie the previous year, compared to one out of five people without disabilities. When asked why, nearly three out of five said they were afraid of being "mistreated" because of their disabilities. Forty percent noted building barriers, such as stairs. Nearly half noted barriers to public transportation. Two-thirds were unemployed, yet an equal number were willing to work.[7] What kept them from taking jobs? The answers included prejudice from employers and physical barriers in the workplace.

college, earn a law degree, and become an attorney whose specialty was disability law. While he had once dressed in jeans, a T-shirt, and a tool belt, the 40-year-old lawyer now wore a suit. One would have to look closely to notice that his upper right arm was paralyzed. Burgdorf was poised to make a major difference in disability law. President Ronald Reagan had appointed him and a dozen other experts to the National Council on the Handicapped, soon renamed the National Council on Disability (NCD). These 13 individuals were meeting in February 1988 in a hotel room in Washington, DC.

There, they would hammer out a piece of national legislation—the Americans with Disabilities Act (ADA).

Serving on the committee with Burgdorf was a "small, frail-looking man," whose appearance might have been misleading to many.[8] Justin Dart Jr., too, had contracted polio the same year as Burgdorf. The disease left his legs paralyzed, so he used a wheelchair. Eighteen years older, he had faced discrimination long before Burgdorf strapped on his tool belt. Dart attended the University of Houston during the early 1950s but had been denied his teaching certification. University officials had thought no one could teach from a wheelchair. With no legal support to challenge that ruling, Dart had given up a teaching career.

The two men, one with his paralyzed arm, the other using a

NO TICKET TO THE MOVIES

Several Americans with disabilities told their stories to the US Congress in support of the ADA. Each revealed a pattern of discrimination against people with disabilities. Nineteen-year-old Lisa Carl was one of them.

One day in 1988, Lisa, who had cerebral palsy, wanted to see a movie at a theater in Tacoma, Washington. But when she approached the ticket window in her wheelchair to buy a ticket, the owner refused to take her money. He was put off by her condition, including her inability to speak clearly.

During her testimony in a US Senate hearing, Lisa spoke of her disappointment: "I was not crying outside, but I was crying inside. I just wanted to be able to watch the movie like everybody else."[9]

People using wheelchairs celebrated the twentieth anniversary of the ADA in 2010.

wheelchair, began to talk of something they both had been dreaming of for years: a comprehensive civil rights act for people with disabilities. President Reagan had given some support to the idea, having created the NCD. But Reagan did not consider their work a priority and did not think the council would make any serious proposals. During one meeting, Burgdorf expressed doubt that anything significant could be done. Many people just were not very interested in people with disabilities. But Dart would not hear it. Ready for action, the man who had spent his adult life in a wheelchair spoke for untold millions of people just like him: "Will we be able to sleep nights if we don't do it? I think we ought to do it no matter what the consequences are."[10]

The members of the council immediately agreed. They had been given an opportunity to bring serious change for the nation's people with disabilities. They could not predict the long months, even years, ahead, and what they would accomplish. Their work would culminate in 1990 with the ADA, a landmark law that would forever change how US society protects individual with disabilities. ●

CHAPTER 2

"LASHED INTO OBEDIENCE"

Throughout human history, there have always been people with different abilities. In some cases, injury or disease leaves a person with a permanent change, as polio changed Burgdorf's life. In other cases, a person is born with a physical or mental difference that causes challenges. In the United States, laws concerning people with disabilities date back to the colonial era, before the country gained its independence from Great Britain.

« **Although life in the North American colonies was difficult, people with disabilities such as New Amsterdam governor Peter Stuyvesant could hold important positions in society.**

Life in the colonies was harsh. It was difficult even for people with no impairments to survive. But those who walked with a limp, were missing an arm, or could not hear well might still be able to do the hard work needed to live on the American frontier. Colonists did not typically discriminate against such individuals. More commonly, communities, led by Christian charity, felt obligated to help care for their neighbors with disabilities.

Early on, colonists passed laws to protect those with disabilities. In the Plymouth Colony, a law was passed in 1636 to provide for those who were no longer "able-bodied." It applied to all men providing military service for the colony. A Massachusetts law passed in 1694 required each town "to take effectual care and make necessary provision for the relief, support and safety of . . . [a] distracted person [person with mental disabilities]."[1]

At first, however, there were few institutions to provide care for people. To fulfill such laws, the local sheriff might believe it necessary to keep a person with a mental impairment in a locked room or even in the jail for their protection. In some communities, the local church might collect money for a poor person with disabilities. Even with the best of intentions, the treatment of individuals with disabilities in colonial

America was never ideal. Some communities, to limit their responsibilities, passed laws against outsiders with disabilities. Such strangers with disabilities or mental illness might be threatened with a whipping if they stayed in a new community too long.

A COLONIAL "CURE" FOR MENTAL ILLNESS

Colonial doctors struggled to care for people with mental illnesses. Several medical books did offer some advice for treating these conditions, none of which worked. The 1747 book *Primitive Physic* offered a strange cure. First, the victim's head was shaved. Then, the doctor applied a mixture of ivy, oil, and white wine to the bald head every 48 hours for three weeks. For a person with mental illness who was violent, the medical manual suggested running cold water over the head. Another suggestion was for the victim to eat a diet of nothing but apples for one month.

Some communities began establishing institutions in the 1700s. Benjamin Franklin helped establish the Pennsylvania Hospital in 1751, which included facilities for treating mental illness. But treatment was not always enlightened. In 1756, hospital officials chained patients to a basement wall. The hospital charged a fee for the people who came to watch the patients exercise in the yard to discourage the visitors.

NEW LAWS IN THE LAND OF THE FREE

When Americans won their independence from Great Britain during the Revolutionary War (1775–1783), many things changed in the new United States. With independence came new responsibilities for citizens, including the right to vote and the need to make their own laws.

Those whom society considered to have disabilities did not often enjoy the fruits of the Revolutionary War or the rights the war produced. Many politicians considered those with disabilities a potential burden to the government. People with disabilities would have to be taken care of, and few families were able to care for their own family members.

This led several states to pass new laws designed to limit the number of persons with disabilities in their state populations. Such laws were not entirely new and had existed in several colonies before the war. These laws applied to those seeking to immigrate to the young United States. They were sometimes called LPC laws, with the initials standing for "likely to become a public charge."

Other laws prejudiced against people with disabilities were passed during the decades following the American Revolution. One type of law targeted voting rights. In

The late 1700s and early 1800s saw the founding of the first institutions for people with disabilities and mental illness, such as the McLean Asylum in Massachusetts.

1821, Massachusetts passed a law to keep any male under another person's guardianship from voting. Virginia passed a law in 1830 denying the vote to anyone "of unsound mind," a blanket term that could have included diagnosable mental illnesses, autism spectrum disorders, speech impairments, intellectual and developmental disabilities, or other conditions.[2] Over the three decades that followed, nearly a dozen additional states passed laws denying the vote to any male thought to be mentally incapable or under a guardianship. These laws were based on the assumption that someone with mental illness or intellectual disabilities could not make wise decisions in voting.

A ONE-WOMAN CAMPAIGN

During the colonial and revolutionary eras, Americans made attempts to improve the lives of less fortunate people, including orphans, the poor, and people with mental illness. Only a few institutions were built, either private or public. By the early 1800s, several states began constructing such facilities, including improved prisons for criminals and almshouses. Although almshouses were essentially places to house the poor, they also became residences for people with intellectual disabilities or mental

SCHOOLS FOR THE DEAF AND BLIND

Reformers of the 1800s also worked to develop new facilities for the treatment and education of the deaf and blind. In 1817, Laurent Clerc and Thomas Hopkins Gallaudet established the American Asylum for the Deaf in Hartford, Connecticut, for the education of deaf children. The school represented the nation's first disability-specific institution. At their school, the deaf could be taught to read and write, read lips, and communicate with sign language. In 1829, another reformer, Samuel Gridley Howe, began an institution for the blind in Massachusetts—Boston's Perkins School for the Blind. The students needed a system to read writing, so Howe invented one that used raised or embossed type read with the fingers. It was called Howe Type or Boston Line Type. Perkins used the Howe system until the invention of braille. Based on variations of dots, braille was an easier system to use. The system of braille was published in 1829 by Louis Braille, a young Frenchman.

illness. The conditions in such facilities were often deplorable. In time, one woman became the face and voice calling for reform.

Dorothea Dix was raised in a home with a distracted, depressive mother and a demanding father. Born in Hampden, Maine, Dix would become a lifelong defender of the downtrodden. At age 12, she left home to live with relatives, including a grandmother and an aunt. An intelligent and inquisitive young woman, Dix began teaching in a private school at age 14. Socially conscious at an early age, she began providing free evening classes for poor children, a rare opportunity at that time. She also wrote books for both children and parents, manuals designed to inform while providing moral instruction.

In 1841, Dix was given a unique opportunity. A local minister asked her to teach a Sunday class for women held in a local jail in East Cambridge, Massachusetts. She agreed and was soon exposed to the shocking conditions of the facility, including a lack of heat. Dix was also appalled to find those held in the jail included people with mental illness and children. Soon, she began a crusade, the first of many, gaining a court order requiring improvements in the jail, including heating.

Having found the conditions of the East Cambridge jail deplorable, Dix soon began investigating other jails and almshouses. Again, what she found was shocking,

Dorothea Dix was a strong voice in the fight for better conditions for people with mental illness in the 1800s.

including the mixing of criminals with people with mental illness. Knowing little about mental illness, Dix read widely on the subject and talked with the leading physicians of her day. Over time, she collected a great deal of firsthand data, finding a lack of food, poorly ventilated buildings, filth, and cruel treatments.

By 1843, she had enough information to prepare a public document. Along with Dr. Samuel Gridley Howe, the director of the Perkins School for the Blind, Dix presented her memorial to the Massachusetts legislature. She described in vivid detail scenes she had witnessed: "I proceed, gentlemen, briefly to call your attention to the present state of . . . persons [with mental illness] confined within this Commonwealth [of Massachusetts] in cages, closets, cellars, stalls, pens! Chained, naked, beaten with rods, and lashed into obedience!"[3] As a direct result of the information Dix presented to the legislators, funds were soon earmarked for the expansion of the State Mental Hospital in Worcester. But Dix's work had only just begun.

Over the next several years, she took her campaign to other states, where she found similar conditions in jails and almshouses. She presented her findings to the New York state legislature in 1844 and to both the New Jersey and Pennsylvania legislatures the following year. New facilities were soon constructed, with Dix providing some of the blueprint. She insisted people with mental illness receive humane, therapeutic treatment and that hospitals be constructed in peaceful, rural settings.

During the American Civil War, Dix continued her humanitarian work, serving as superintendent of US Army nurses. After the war, Dix returned to her work in support of people with mental illness but had little new success.

The following excerpt is from Dorothea Dix's speech "Memorial to the Massachusetts Legislature" (1843), in which she describes the poor treatment of people with mental illness in that state:

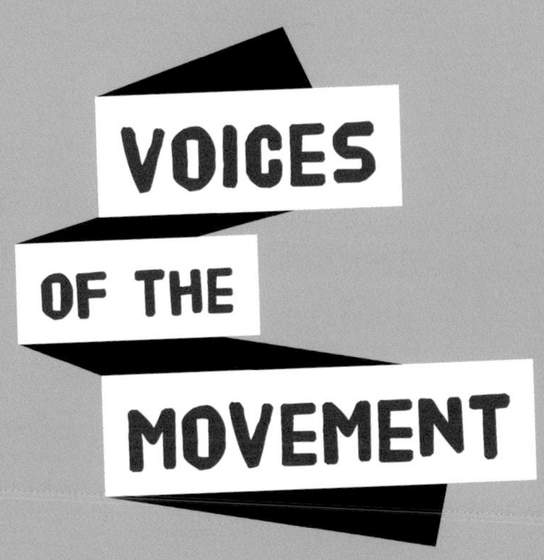

"I tell what I have seen—painful and shocking as the details often are—that from them you may feel more deeply the imperative obligation . . . to prevent . . . a repetition or continuance of such outrages upon humanity. . . . I offer the following extracts from my Note-book and Journal:

. . . Lincoln. A woman in a cage. Medford. One idiotic subject chained, and one in a close stall for seventeen years. Pepperell. One often doubly chained, hand and foot; another violent; several peaceable now. Brookfield. One man caged, comfortable. Granville. One often closely confined; now losing the use of his limbs from want of exercise. . . . Lenox. Two in the jail, against whose unfit condition there the jailer protests. . . . I give a few illustrations; but description fades before reality."[4]

States that had made improvements and built better facilities in earlier decades had often let the conditions in their state-run hospitals deteriorate. Yet, by her death in 1887, no American had done more in support of people with mental illness than Dix. ●

Even in the 1940s, a century after Dix's campaign began, people with mental illness living in asylums were still at times strapped down to their beds. »

CHAPTER 3

THE RISE OF DISABILITY INSTITUTIONS

During the 1860s, the people of the United States went to war with one another. More than 600,000 Americans—including blue-clad Northerners and gray-clad Southerners—were killed during the American Civil War (1861–1865).[1] In addition, tens of thousands of men were wounded, many of whom lost limbs or eyes or suffered other permanent injuries. Veterans with

« **The Civil War left many men with missing limbs or other injuries. Lucius Fairchild lost an arm at the Battle of Gettysburg and later became governor of Wisconsin.**

disabilities had trouble finding jobs. But with the increase in photography, wounded veterans and veterans with disabilities could not be ignored. At least 45,000 emerged from the war with one or more limbs amputated.[2] Pictures showed them legless, armless, or otherwise disfigured.

With so many injuries and amputations, a new industry expanded, providing artificial limbs and other adaptive devices for wounded veterans. In 1866, in the state of Mississippi, for example, 20 percent of the state's income was spent providing artificial limbs to its war veterans.[3] Enterprising inventors made improvements in prostheses. The first wheelchair patent was issued in 1869. Such innovations helped improve life for the war's veterans as well as the civilian population.

However, with so many disfigured men on the streets, cities began passing "ugly laws." San Francisco, California, passed such a law in 1867. It prohibited "any person who is diseased, maimed, mutilated, or in any way deformed so as to be an unsightly or disgusting object" from being seen on the city's streets.[4] Other cities, such as Chicago, Illinois, passed similar laws. In Portland, Oregon, the law forbade "any crippled, maimed, or deformed person" from panhandling in public places.[5] The point of such laws was to remove those with disabilities from public view. The message was clear: out of sight, out of mind.

NEW INNOVATIONS IN PROSTHESES

The Civil War produced many veterans with disabilities. As a result, companies saw a new market for prostheses and special devices for people with war-related disabilities. The list of new prostheses covered every injury from head to foot. Adaptive equipment included special walking canes, braces, glass eyes, and other devices.

Some devices were created by the people with the disabilities themselves. One Civil War veteran, Samuel A. Craig, had been wounded in the face and neck. He fashioned a homemade wax plate to fit into his mouth. "By fixing the wax plate over the hole in the roof of my mouth, I was enabled to talk and drink soup," Craig explained.[6] The plate served another purpose—Craig was able to remain in uniform and continue his service as a soldier. The wars of the 1900s would see the invention of many more prostheses and assistive devices.

CHANGES IN INSTITUTIONS

During the half century following the Civil War, schools for the deaf and blind increased dramatically in number. Many Americans placed a new emphasis on education during the latter decades of the 1800s, and those with disabilities believed education could improve their lives as well. In 1864, the US Congress established the National Deaf-Mute College. Thirty years later, it was renamed Gallaudet College, to honor Thomas Gallaudet's groundbreaking efforts

President Abraham Lincoln signed the order establishing Gallaudet College.

in establishing his American Asylum for the Deaf back in 1817. By 1900, more than 130 residential schools for the deaf had been established.[7]

FIRST FEMALE GRADUATE

In 1893, Agatha Tiegel became the first female graduate from Gallaudet. Tiegel had become deaf at the age of seven when she contracted spinal meningitis. While at Gallaudet, she was the youngest of the eight women attending. Tiegel went on to teach at the Minnesota School for the Deaf, where she met and married Olof Hanson, a native Swede and graduate of the Minnesota institution. By 1910, he was president of the National Association of the Deaf. For many years, Agatha Tiegel Hanson and her husband remained leaders in the deaf community.

Schools were also founded for students with other disabilities. By 1900, there were 31 institutions for the blind and more than a dozen schools for those with intellectual or developmental disabilities, what was often called "feeble-mindedness" at the time.[8] All these institutions provided hope for people with disabilities in the United States. However, a majority of those with disabilities were either kept at home or lived in asylums and state-run homes for the poor.

Dix had planted seeds during the 1840s that had taken dramatic root by the 1860s and 1870s. Her call for better facilities for people with mental illnesses led to many states building new facilities. Many were constructed in rural settings where land was cheaper. And many of these facilities were built using the Kirkbride Plan.

Originally the superintendent of the Philadelphia Hospital for the Insane, Dr. Thomas Story Kirkbride was an early American advocate for a new type of asylum. Kirkbride's asylum plan called for a central administration building with two multistory wings, one coming off each side. In Kirkbride's asylums, patients would be segregated by gender and the type of illness they had. Patients could go outside and enjoy therapeutic fresh air and sunshine.

Not everyone who needed such treatment was able to get help. Some did not know facilities were available to them. Some families refused to admit that a relative might have a mental illness. Shockingly, others were still locked away in prisons, either undiagnosed or misdiagnosed. For them, little had changed in nearly a century. Even in the 2010s, the rate of mental illness in prisons is very high.

THE PROGRESSIVE ERA

During the first 20 years of the 1900s, Americans experienced an era of much social and political change. This period came to be known as the Progressive Era. Significant numbers of people supported political reforms, including new laws protecting workers, women, children, and others. Some Progressive laws helped those who sustained disabilities due to work accidents. New laws establishing worker's compensation spread across the country. This meant those sustaining injuries or

NO IMMIGRANTS WITH DISABILITIES ALLOWED

A great wave of immigrants from Europe came to the United States during the decades before and after 1900. New federal laws kept out people with disabilities. The Immigration Act of 1882 denied entrance to any "lunatic, idiot, or any person unable to take care of himself or herself without becoming a public charge."[9] Additional national laws denying individuals with disabilities immigration were passed regularly between 1890 and 1910. A 1917 law directed officials to keep out any immigrants with "any mental abnormality . . . which justifies the statement that the alien is mentally defective."[10]

Since many immigrants did not speak English, it was sometimes difficult for officials to even communicate with them. Deciding who was "mentally defective" was merely one official's opinion. Decisions were sometimes based on little more than "odd" facial expressions, "strange" mannerisms, or a "curious" style of clothing. Some immigrants were turned away for little more than having what officials described as a "poor physique."[11]

disabilities at work were to be paid for their injuries.

Many new institutions and schools had been established for people with disabilities during the decades leading up to 1900. Progressives began retooling some of those institutions. Some experts suggested the institutions for people with disabilities should be organized differently, a change called "the colony plan." One expert, Dr. William Spratling, ran a facility in Sonyea, New York, for people with epilepsy. He compared the plan to creating a bee colony: "The innumerable hives picturesquely scattered

Progressive reformer Lewis W. Hine photographed this teenager who lost his arm in a factory accident in 1908 and received no compensation from his employers.

through sweet smelling fields . . . stand, in colony life, for contented and happy homes."[12]

In the colony plan, the facility and grounds included an administrative building at its hub. Paths radiated out from the center, like the spokes of a wheel, leading to a

FORCED STERILIZATION

Amid the positive changes of the early 1900s, however, a dark idea began targeting some Americans with disabilities: forced sterilization. Some people, even some scientists and doctors, believed people with physical disabilities should not be allowed to have children. The thought was that those with disabilities might also suffer from mental or moral "defects." Such sterilization laws were often written broadly. They might apply to anyone who had intellectual or mental disabilities, visual or hearing impairments, epilepsy, any other kind of physical disability, orphans, the homeless, or poor people.

Legal challenges arose. But a 1927 US Supreme Court decision, *Buck v. Bell*, generally upheld sterilization laws. After 1900 and as late as the 1960s, more than 65,000 Americans with disabilities were the victims of forced sterilization.[14]

system of "cottages." Each cottage might house as many as 30 to 40 residents.[13] Each provided a "home" of sorts for those with similar disabilities. However, the colony plan seemed like a step backward to critics. Earlier institutions had attempted to educate and even help transition people with disabilities back into society. The colony plan was an attempt to remove people with disabilities from society. Those who did not approve called the plan a friendlier place to warehouse people with disabilities. ●

Patients at a New York City institution for people with mental illness occupied their time with basket weaving. »

CHAPTER 4

"JOBS, NOT TIN CUPS"

Just as the Civil War had brought change to the lives of people with disabilities, especially veterans, so did World War I (1914–1918). Again, the prosthetics industry produced new devices for those who needed artificial limbs or even facial reconstruction. As after the Civil War, many Americans were forced to view people with disabilities differently. Veterans of World War I with disabilities were treated with more respect because they

« **This false eye was attached to eyeglasses to cover a World War I veteran's missing eye.**

had been injured serving their country. In the eyes of many Americans, a "crippled" veteran (that is, a veteran with a mobility impairment) was a "good" person with disabilities, while a nonveteran person with disabilities might be considered a second-class citizen.

Rehabilitation experts called for programs to provide vocational training for veterans. The National Defense Act of 1916, the Smith-Hughes Act of 1917, and the Smith-Sears Veterans' Rehabilitation Act of 1918 all created vocational training programs. After the war, Red Cross posters were plastered across the country in support of businesses hiring veterans with disabilities. One 1919

DISABLED AMERICAN VETERANS

In 1920, World War I veterans founded the Disabled American Veterans, known popularly as the DAV. The group remained at the center of the struggle for veterans injured by the war through the 1920s. By 1932, the nonprofit organization was designated by Congress as "the official voice of the nation's wartime disabled veterans."[1]

The organization is still going strong, and in the 2010s, membership stood at 1.2 million.[2] Health care and mental health care for veterans, suicide prevention, and other veterans' benefits are among the most important political issues for the group.

The Red Cross advertised government rehabilitation programs for veterans after World War I.

poster insisted, "The man profitably employed is no longer handicapped."[3]

The door to vocational training had been opened. More Americans began considering the possibilities for the nation's people with disabilities. It was not long before the opportunities for such training were made available to the larger community of people with disabilities. In 1920, Congress passed the Smith-Fess Act. This law provided vocational training to civilians with disabilities who had not served in the military. By 1922, 34 states had created their own state-level vocational rehabilitation programs.[4] Still, many employers chose not to hire workers with disabilities, whether they were veterans or not.

CHALLENGES OF THE GREAT DEPRESSION

In October 1929, the stock market crashed, causing the nation's economy to free-fall into a deep depression. Unemployment reached an all-time high. The times were difficult for a vast majority of Americans, whether they had disabilities or not.

Throughout the 1930s, even as Americans struggled through the Great Depression, the nation's people with disabilities made further advances. Those with disabilities engaged in new levels of activism as they campaigned for greater recognition and opportunities. The government would respond to some of their demands by changing federal policy.

In 1932, the nation elected a new president. Franklin Delano Roosevelt was a wealthy New York politician. He campaigned that fall on a platform promising a “new deal” for all Americans. He was determined to fight the effects of the devastating depression. Following his inauguration in March 1933, with the aid of Congress he launched a sweeping package of policies designed to help the nation’s economy recover. For people with disabilities in the United States, there were opportunities ahead.

President Roosevelt himself lived with a disability. In 1921, in his late thirties, he had contracted polio and lost the use of his legs. In private, Roosevelt used a wheelchair. But he did not want the public to know he was paralyzed from the waist down, so in public, he left his wheelchair at home. He walked using a set of braces on his legs, usually with someone walking alongside him.

THE NEW DEAL

Roosevelt and Congress quickly created a number of new federal agencies, each one targeting a problem linked to the Great Depression. There were new relief programs providing funds for families in need. The Civilian Conservation Corps helped put young men to work on federal land, building roads, park buildings, and other infrastructure. Job programs, such as the Public Works Administration and the Works Progress Administration, helped provide temporary work for men and women ranging from heavy construction to art projects.

President Roosevelt rarely allowed himself to be photographed on crutches or in a wheelchair.

But these and other agencies did little to provide people with disabilities with jobs and other assistance. In the spring of 1935, New Yorkers with disabilities protested outside the city's Emergency Relief Bureau. The angry protesters carried signs reading "We Don't Want Tin Cups. We Want Jobs" and "We Are Lame But We Can

THE DEAF AND THE GREAT DEPRESSION

The deaf community faced a difficult time during the Great Depression. The deaf had made great strides during previous decades, forming various support organizations, including the National Fraternal Society of the Deaf, at the turn of the century. New schools had been established during the 1920s. But the Great Depression represented a step backward for deaf individuals. Between 1929 and 1935, 44 percent of deaf individuals who had jobs before the stock market crash lost them.[7]

Since government-financed New Deal programs considered people with disabilities "unemployable," jobs did not come easily. But some gains were made. Largely through the efforts of the National Association of the Deaf, exceptions were made for the deaf in hiring practices carried out by the Works Progress Administration by 1938. Yet the gains were temporary. By the following year, policies changed and the deaf were again considered unemployable.

Work."[5] They were tired of government programs that treated nearly all individuals with disabilities as unemployable.

By 1935, these protesters organized themselves and other people with disabilities into the League of the Physically Handicapped. This early activist organization supported people with disabilities. An early flyer included one of the group's demands: "We *demand* the government recognize its obligation to make adequate provisions for handicapped people in the Works Relief Program."[6]

But little changed immediately in the government's employment practices.

However, the organization did not give up. For more than 40 years, the League of the Physically Handicapped continued fighting discrimination against people with disabilities. The grassroots organization studied and practiced new ways to advance the rights of Americans with disabilities, especially through the legal system. Members of the group understood the laws of the United States would have to be changed before anything resembling true equality for people with disabilities would ever be achieved.

DOGS, THE BLIND'S BEST FRIEND

Today, the blind rely on specially trained dogs to help them achieve fuller mobility. But there was a time when dogs and the blind did not go hand in hand. The poison gas used in World War I led to an influx of veterans who lost their sight. After the war, seeing-eye dogs were first used in Germany to lead blind war veterans. The word spread, and soon they were in use to aid blind civilians.

In 1926, Dorothy Harrison Eustis, a wealthy American woman, visited a German school that specialized in training dogs for the blind. The following year, she wrote an article about the school and its trained dogs for the popular magazine *Saturday Evening Post*. Morris Frank, a recently blinded young American, learned of the article and was convinced dogs could serve blind individuals in a unique way. By 1929, Eustis and Frank had founded The Seeing Eye, the first US training school for guide dogs.

NEW LAWS SUPPORTING PEOPLE WITH DISABILITIES

During most of the 1930s, the federal government did not take serious steps to provide employment opportunities for people with disabilities. But laws were passed to provide them some security. In January 1935, in an address to Congress, President Roosevelt called for new laws to provide for various groups of Americans, including older citizens, poor children, and those with physical disabilities. The result was the Economic Security Bill, which created the framework for three federal programs: welfare, unemployment compensation, and old-age insurance.

Through the summer of 1935, the proposed bill went through various changes, only to emerge as the Social Security Act. The new law was signed by Roosevelt on August 14, 1935. The states became responsible for unemployment payments and welfare programs, although the federal government provided most of the money.

The Social Security Act of 1935 accomplished even more. For the first time in US history, vocational rehabilitation achieved permanent authority and funding as a government program. Millions of federal dollars were set aside for vocational rehabilitation and for caring for children with disabilities. The federal government was dedicating more resources and money to the nation's people with disabilities than ever before.

However, only two groups of persons with disabilities immediately received cash benefits from the 1935 law, the blind and children with disabilities. In 1943, Congress passed the Barden-LaFollette Act, which provided federal money for several types of medical and reconstructive services that had never been covered by previous federal rehab programs. Perhaps even more important, the new law provided coverage for people with mental illnesses or intellectual disabilities.

It took longer to enact a disability insurance program, partially because it was difficult to define disability and put in

WHITE CANES AND THE LIONS CLUB

Most Americans are accustomed to seeing blind individuals walking with special canes. These canes came into popular use through the passage of the nation's first White Cane Law in 1930. The law had become a favorite cause of the Lion's Club, a men's social group. The Peoria, Illinois, chapter helped see passage of a city ordinance in 1930 that required all motorists to yield to anyone carrying a white cane signaling they were blind. Following this success, members of the Lions Club launched a national campaign for the passage of similar laws in other states.

The canes have since proven an important aid to the blind. By tapping them on pavement, blind individuals can signal their presence on the street. The tapping also produces echoes that help the blind interpret their surroundings.

place a system for determining who qualified for benefits. An amendment to the Social Security Act in 1950 began providing the first benefits. Over time, many amendments tweaked the definition of disability and adjusted the criteria used to determine the benefits received by people with disabilities and their families. ●

Through the 1930s, people with disabilities integrated themselves more into society as the government passed laws and dedicated more money to aid them. »

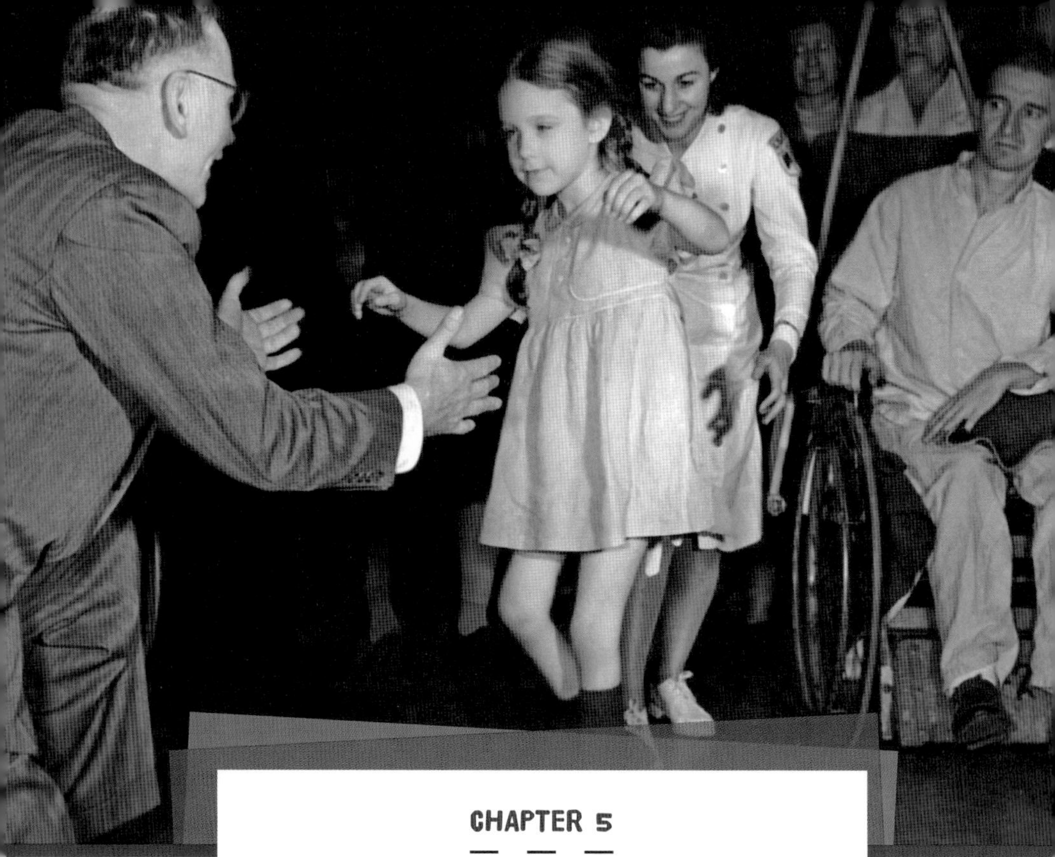

CHAPTER 5

POLIO, WAR, AND NEW VIEWS

Life for many of the country's people with disabilities continued to be a struggle. The majority of people continued practicing discrimination against people with disabilities. Often this discrimination was based in society's lack of understanding about disabilities and the people who lived with them. By the time of the Great Depression, one disease was causing some Americans to

« **The polio epidemic led more Americans to become activists for disability rights.**

take a new look at what it meant to live with disabilities. That disease was polio.

Polio survivors belonged to every class and social group in the country. Many emerged from the experience using a wheelchair, crutches, or leg braces. No longer could Americans simply look the other way. A new era of activism was soon on the rise. The March of Dimes campaign, intended to support young polio victims, was founded in 1938. Other activists sought to expose the often poor conditions found in the country's institutions for

ROOSEVELT AND THE MARCH OF DIMES

During his presidency, Franklin Roosevelt helped establish the National Foundation for Infantile Paralysis. The organization was privately funded. It provided leg braces, wheelchairs, and other devices to young people struggling with polio whose families could not afford such equipment themselves. Funds were also used to pay for polio prevention and research.

Within a few years of its founding, the NFIP would be renamed the March of Dimes. Booths were set up in cities where children could drop dimes in slots. The organization encouraged schoolchildren to collect dimes to help those with polio. In one campaign, kids sent in their dimes to help build a swimming pool so Roosevelt could swim at the White House. Since 1946, Roosevelt's image has been on the face of the dime as a tribute to his contributions to the March of Dimes.

people with disabilities, including mental hospitals and psychiatric institutions.

WORLD WAR II

Just as earlier US wars had brought changes for people with disabilities, so did World War II (1939–1945). The federal government shifted its fight from battling the Great Depression to opposing Germany, Italy, and Japan, which attacked a US military base in Hawaii in December 1941. Government wartime employment policies were still largely unfriendly toward people with disabilities. But as the war continued, manpower shortages worsened. Government employment of people with disabilities skyrocketed during the war from approximately 30,000 in 1940 to ten times that figure by 1945. A mindset against

THE DANGERS OF WAR

As with all US wars, conflicts such as World War II produced tens of thousands of veterans who returned home with disabilities due to wounds and military-related accidents. But there were other casualties as well. Back in the United States, the war put millions of people to work in wartime industry. These workers produced everything from bullets to trucks to ships. Many industry-related jobs were dangerous. The result was a large number of accidents leading to disabilities. As one historian would later write: "During the first few years of the Second World War, it was safer for Americans to be on the battlefront than it was for them to work on the home front in the arsenal of democracy."[1]

World War II veterans welcomed government programs and social activities to help them reintegrate into society.

people with disabilities seemed to have been changed. Between 1940 and 1950 the US government employed nearly 2 million workers with disabilities.[2] During those same years, private businesses also chose to hire individuals with disabilities more frequently.

Once again, war brought injury and disability to many. Industrial accidents in the United States during the war also contributed to injuries and disabilities. New government programs were created for individuals with war-related disabilities. These included a new vocational training program as part of the Barden-LaFollette Act of 1943. This act also provided for physical rehabilitation services and granted opportunities for individuals to attend specialized schools, colleges, and universities.

But a new call was going out on behalf of Americans with disabilities. Activists pushed for a new legal definition of disability. People with disabilities, whether they received their disability through war, accident, or circumstance of birth, all deserved full and equal rights, including employment and education opportunities, and access to all places in the United States, both public and private. Having a disability had become a civil rights issue more than ever before.

WORLD WAR II AND MENTAL HOSPITALS

World War II also changed the state of mental hospitals in the United States. During the war, men unwilling to fight for philosophical or religious reasons could claim conscientious objector status. They were still required to serve, however. One way they contributed to the war effort was working in mental hospitals across the country. In all, approximately 3,000 conscientious objectors (COs) worked in 62 such facilities.[3]

What they often found in these institutions were poor living conditions and substandard care. Some COs cooperated with writers for *Life* magazine and other publications to expose these awful conditions. A group of COs formed a new organization to support those in mental institutions—the National Mental Health Foundation.

In 1950, the organization joined together with National Committee for Mental Hygiene and the Psychiatric Foundation. The new organization became the National Association for Mental Health. The group is still an important advocacy organization supporting mental health issues.

PAUL STRACHAN AND THE AFPH

During and after World War II, organizations supporting people with disabilities were more active than ever. Paul Strachan, a labor union organizer, founded the American Federation of the Physically Handicapped (AFPH) in 1942.

Strachan, "tall, deaf, and impassioned," was extremely effective in using his organizational talents to achieve real results in disability rights.[4] While most earlier organizations supporting people with disabilities had been specific to one disability such as blindness or deafness, Strachan insisted his organization span across all disabilities. He drew members who had amputated limbs, diabetes, hearing impairments, vision impairments, epilepsy, polio, and other conditions.

Strachan was an early proponent of what would become known as the "rights model of disability"—the belief that people with disabilities should have the same rights as everyone else.[5] This model of thought called for society to adapt to the needs of individuals with disabilities rather than asking the individual to make do or do without. Strachan lobbied for civil rights legislation to protect individuals with disabilities from discrimination and support the hiring of people with disabilities.

His call was for the public to view people with disabilities positively. "WHY, or WHY is it," he asked,

PAUL STRACHAN: A DEDICATED ACTIVIST

Disability advocate Paul Strachan was born in Perry, Michigan, in February 1892. When World War I opened, Strachan tried to enlist but was turned down due to poor hearing. During the war, he established the Bureau of War Risk Insurance.

Following the war, he helped organize a union of government employees, which led to an interest in vocational training. He was soon helping craft bills providing vocational training for veterans and others. In 1942, he organized the American Federation of the Physically Handicapped. Soon, his organization boasted chapters across the country.

Not long after, Strachan was injured in an auto accident. During his lengthy recovery, he began envisioning the National Employ the Physically Handicapped Week. Some time would pass before Congress gave his idea national recognition, but once the event finally happened in 1945, it was a success. Strachan continued to work on behalf of people with disabilities until his retirement in 1952.

"there still exists this unreasoning, unjust prejudice against millions of Handicapped people? Why cannot Industry, and the public . . . realize that we, too, aspire to the comforts, the feeling of security that comes from fair recognition of our rights as citizens?"[6]

Strachan and the AFPH called for accessible buildings and better worker safety. He worked with the Department of Labor and labor unions to craft new federal laws supporting people with disabilities and their rights. He campaigned on behalf of World War II veterans, pushing for more job opportunities

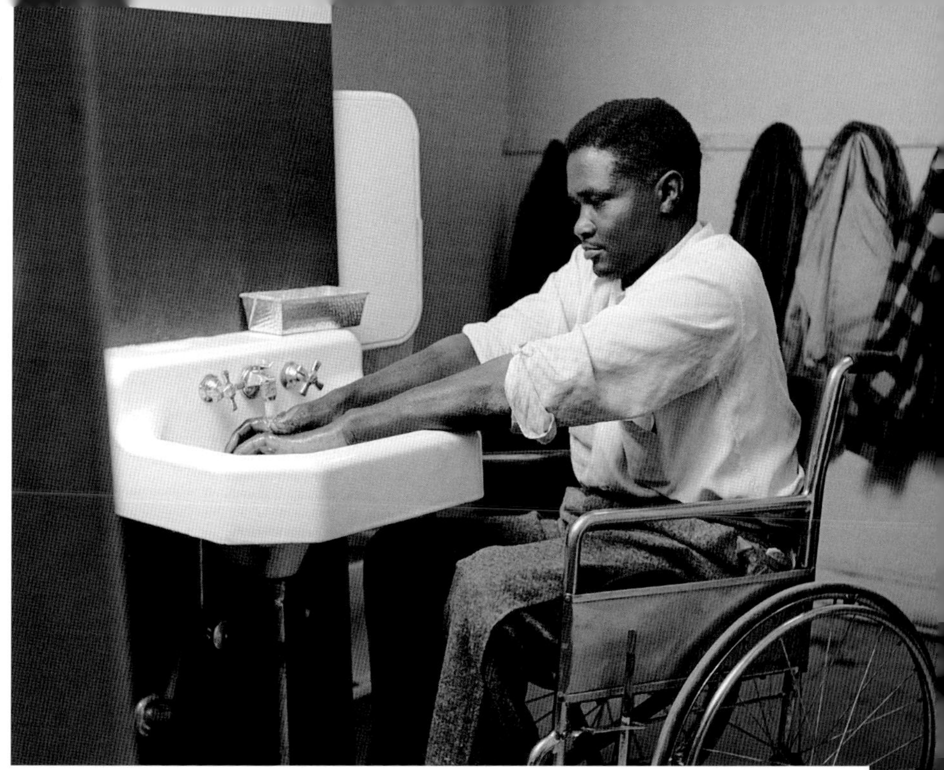

The postwar period saw an increase in facilities designed for accessibility, though such accommodations were still rare.

and government training. Strachan was responsible for the establishment of a National Employ the Physically Handicapped Week in 1945. He served on the President's Committee on the Handicapped until 1952.

World War II had delivered more rehabilitation legislation, most of which was designed to specifically help war veterans. The 1950s saw an additional round of rehab laws as well, including the Vocational Rehabilitation Amendments of 1954. These laws were designed not only to help people with disabilities gain mobility or a better way of life. They were intended to help people with disabilities move more freely in the mainstream of society. ●

CHAPTER 6

THE INDEPENDENT LIVING MOVEMENT

In the years following the end of World War II, the course of the disability movement changed dramatically. Advocates for people with disabilities began using, as never before, language that emphasized human rights, equality, and discrimination. No longer were people with disabilities going to accept social attitudes that expected them to simply keep quiet, keep out of sight, and stay to themselves. Individuals with

« **In the postwar period, people with mental illness or developmental disabilities were still often sent to institutions to be forgotten.**

disabilities were gearing up for a greater place in society and were expecting society to adjust to them, rather than the other way around. Prejudice and discrimination toward them were things many Americans with disabilities had previously come to accept as a way of life for themselves—but no longer.

MORE REHABILITATION LAWS

To help individuals with disabilities prepare themselves for life in mainstream society, the government developed more rehabilitation programs. The two world wars, plus the Great Depression, had seriously altered the role of government in the lives of people with disabilities. A long list of rehab services was needed.

One such law was passed during the administration

CHANGING MODELS OF DISABILITY

In the past, society understood disability through what might be called a medical model of disability. Through this lens, a person with disabilities is seen as needing to be fixed so he or she can fit into society—"disabilities are impairments to be cured through medical intervention."[1] In contrast, the social model of disability views disability as a construction of society. The individual and his or her disability is not the problem; rather, society is the problem unless it adapts to the needs of all its members.

of President Lyndon B. Johnson. His massive package of social programs, called the Great Society, included the Vocational Rehabilitation Amendments of 1965. Also passed in 1965, Medicare and Medicaid provided health insurance for Americans considered "disabled." These programs for people with disabilities were part of President Johnson's War on Poverty. The new legislation meant more money spent on individuals with disabilities, plus new vocational rehab services. Soon followed the 1968 Vocational Rehabilitation Act Amendments, which required states to set aside money for vocational training for youth with disabilities.

ENROLLING AT BERKELEY

One of the important aspects of the activism during the 1960s was the independent living movement. An important starting point for the movement took place at the University of California, Berkeley, in 1962. That same year, James Meredith, an African American, fought and won the right to enroll in the University of Mississippi. Previously, school officials had not allowed African-American students to attend the university. Similarly, students with disabilities were beginning to speak up.

At UC Berkeley that year, Edward Roberts sued college officials to allow him to enroll. Meredith had contracted polio earlier in life and had faced prejudice before. As a high school student, his principal had not allowed him to graduate because he had not taken a gym class. Meredith used a wheelchair and an iron lung. The California Department of Rehabilitation had turned him down to receive college financial aid. The agency believed he would not pay back his aid money because he would never be able to hold a job.

Roberts won his case, but university officials did not make things easy for him. He was denied a dorm room because none could accommodate his iron lung. He had to live in the university infirmary instead. But Roberts had

DISABILITY ACTIVISTS AND CIVIL RIGHTS

The disabilities movement found new energy in the civil rights movement. The movement focused on attaining civil rights for the nation's minorities, especially African Americans. During the 1950s and early 1960s, major events pushed the country closer to racial equality. The organized efforts by the African-American community and its supporters focused on public protest, marches, nonviolence, and careful planning and organization.

In the end, these actions led to new federal laws that worked to destroy segregation. The Civil Rights Act of 1964 promised equal rights in employment, education, and public accommodations. The Voting Rights Act of 1965 gave African Americans and other minorities greater access to the vote. In 1968, the Civil Rights Act, also called the Fair Housing Act, guaranteed equal housing access. Through these laws, a significant minority group was promised equality and protection against discrimination. The disability movement took several pages from the civil rights movement playbook.

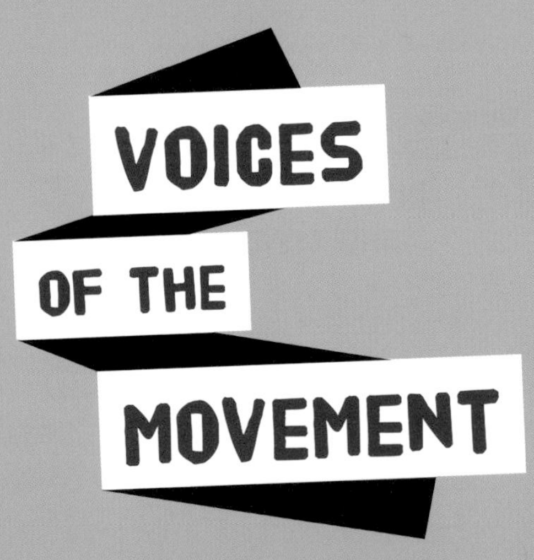

Once Edward Roberts broke the barrier by gaining the right to attend UC Berkeley in 1962, the campus became a magnet for other students with disabilities. Student Cathrine Louisa Caulfield began attending the university in 1968. She was the first female roommate in the infirmary where the students with disabilities lived. She carried fond memories living at the university's third-floor Cowell Hospital "dorm" throughout her life, until her death in 2003. In an interview, she recalled the following:

"Living at Cowell was very exciting and very busy. We were all going to school. In the evenings we would get together and discuss everything! We had to attend to our immediate needs, like privacy, curfews, attendants, and how to deal with the nurses from the second floor. . . . Berkeley was the place to be then. We were attending one of the greatest universities in the world. . . . It was a crazy, exciting time and the disabled movement was part of that time."[2]

opened the door, and by his sophomore year, additional students with disabilities were allowed to enroll. They lived on the infirmary's third floor, which soon became known as the "Rolling Quads" because of the number of students living there who used wheelchairs.

These students had won one battle, and they were ready for others. The UC students with disabilities soon organized the Disabled Students' Program (DSP). The group members campaigned and won the right to access all parts of the Berkeley campus. School officials had to remodel buildings so there were no barriers to wheelchair access. By 1972, the Berkeley campus was home to the Center for Independent Living, an advocacy organization for people with disabilities.

Roberts graduated and got a job, despite the California Department of Rehabilitation's earlier prediction he would never be employed. Perhaps ironically, Roberts would later serve as the agency's director.

LIVING INDEPENDENTLY

The idea of independent living began to spread across the country. Independent living is more than just living alone. For more than 150 years, the trend of support for Americans with disabilities had been the development of institutions. There had been schools for the blind and the deaf. Often these institutions had provided sanctuary and

Eunice Kennedy Shriver, a supporter of rights for people with disabilities, visited students at the Margaret Chapman School in Hawthorne, New York, in 1975.

security for people with disabilities. But these institutions typically had removed individuals with disabilities from the larger society. Now, a new move away from institutions was taking place.

The movement focused on helping create mini-worlds in which individuals could live without relying on institutions. Through changes brought about by the independent living movement, people with disabilities could lead lives similar to those without disabilities. During the 1970s and 1980s, activists supporting independent living managed to see the removal of transportation and architectural barriers. They supported anything and everything that might make the lives of Americans with disabilities easier and more independent. Supporters provided legal assistance, peer counseling,

Eunice Kennedy Shriver, sister to President John F. Kennedy, began the Special Olympics movement in 1962. She discusses the challenges facing children with mental disabilities and their parents in a 1962 issue of the *Saturday Evening Post*.

"We are just coming out of the dark ages in our handling of this serious national problem. Even within the last several years, there have been known instances where families have committed . . . infants [with mental disabilities] to institutions before they were a month old—and ran obituaries in the local papers to spread the belief that they were dead. In this era of atom-splitting and wonder drugs and technological advance, it is still widely assumed—even among some medical people—that the future for [people with mental disabilities] is hopeless. . . . Unless a person has had intimate contact with [people with mental disabilities] . . . the mind's-eye impressions are likely to be deeply prejudiced."[3]

various types of training, and even wheelchair repair. As never before, individuals with disabilities were able to lead fuller lives. Independent living for adults with disabilities became the new norm.

The numbers begin to paint the picture. Between 1965 and 1980, the number of individuals with disabilities in US institutions dropped by 60 percent, from 475,000 to 138,000.[4] Earlier, patients with disabilities had spent many years, if not their entire lives, in an institution. Following 1970, many patients were spending a mere matter of weeks or days in institutions. Activist and teacher Dr. Burton Blatt was instrumental in this change. He raised awareness of the inhumane conditions in

INDEPENDENT LIVING FACILITIES

Among the facilities developing in the 1960s were three that would become extremely popular—independent living centers, community mental health centers, and group homes.

Independent living centers are cross-disability, community-based organizations run by and serving people with all types of disabilities. The purpose of these centers is to give people with disabilities the support they need to live their lives as they wish.

A community mental health center is a facility available to someone in need of counseling or mental health services. A group home is a compact, supervised residential facility, usually designed for people with mental illnesses. Residents live together, completing daily chores, and are free to come and go voluntarily.

Activists in New York protested outside the governor's office over cuts to education and rehabilitation programs in the state in 1969.

some institutions through his book *Christmas in Purgatory*, a photo exposé.

Independent living opportunities were varied and included such places as independent living centers, community mental health centers, and group homes. But independent living facilities could not be found everywhere in the United States. Sometimes, individuals with disabilities living independently were able to do so only with family support or some other source of funding. There remained tens of thousands without support. Some were homeless. Others, through dire circumstances, landed in jails and even prisons—especially people with mental illnesses. Circumstances were still short of perfect for many Americans with disabilities. ●

CHAPTER 7

ACTIVISTS AND SECTION 504

One challenge faced by people with physical disabilities is mobility. Historically, those who had difficulty walking or who used a wheelchair often found buildings difficult to maneuver or impossible to enter. Few laws required buildings, public or private, to be constructed with people with physical disabilities in mind. In 1961, two groups proposed model building codes designed to take away many of the barriers—the

« **Protesters outside the US Capitol in 1972 called for an "equal rights proclamation" for people with disabilities, including accessible buildings and public transportation.**

National Society for Crippled Children and Adults (today called Easter Seals) and the President's Commission on Employment of the Handicapped. Some referred to the proposal as "the Declaration of Independence for the Handicapped."[1]

In 1968, Congress passed the Architectural Barriers Act. One individual played a significant role in bringing about this important piece of legislation. Hugh Gallagher was a legislative aide to Alaskan Senator Bob Bartlett. Since surviving polio at the age of 19, Gallagher had used a

EASTER SEALS

Easter Seals is one of the most important private organizations supporting children and adults with disabilities. It provides services through the United States, Canada, Australia, and Puerto Rico.

Ohio businessman Edgar Allen founded the organization. After his son was killed in a streetcar accident in 1907, Allen raised funds to build a new hospital. Once the hospital was in operation, Allen was appalled to learn children with disabilities were not treated well. This led Allen to establish the National Society for Crippled Children in 1919.

A fund-raising campaign was organized in 1934. Special stamps called "seals" were sold to the public. These seals were affixed to envelopes, in addition to real stamps, as a show of support. The National Society for Crippled Children continued the "seals" campaign as an annual fund-raiser. By 1967, the Easter "seal" was so well known officials renamed the organization Easter Seals.

Hugh Gallagher, ***second from left*****, was instrumental in the passage of the Architectural Barriers Act.**

wheelchair. Working in Washington, DC, he constantly found federal buildings difficult to enter. Through his campaign and with the support of many others, a federal commission was established to examine the issue of architectural barriers. The 1968 act was the first step in eliminating this problem. Gallagher would later describe what the new law meant to him: "I wanted it to be simple. I wanted accessibility to be one of the items on the checklist of designers and builders."[2]

The law required that any new buildings, as well as those remodeled with federal dollars, would have to be physically accessible. The law was groundbreaking. It signaled the direction of activism during the years to follow.

THE REHABILITATION ACT

Five years later came the passage of the Rehabilitation Act of 1973. Just as earlier legislation had been created following previous wars, this new law was sparked by the needs of veterans of the Vietnam War (1955–1975) with disabilities.

Passing the Rehabilitation Act of 1973 was not an easy victory. In 1972, Congress began looking at vocational rehabilitation legislation differently than in earlier years. Such groups as the National Rehabilitation Association, with assistance in Congress from Senator Alan Cranston of California and Representative John Brademas of Indiana, pushed for passage of the Rehabilitation Act. The act gave priority to serving people with severe disabilities. It supported independent living services intended to integrate people with disabilities into society more completely.

The 1972 bill passed Congress and reached the desk of President Richard Nixon. He did not sign the bill. But Congress would not surrender the cause. In March 1973, a similar bill was passed. Congress recognized pressure from the disability rights activist organization Disabled in Action (DIA). Its members and others protested at the Lincoln Memorial in Washington, DC.

DISABLED IN ACTION

The DIA was founded in 1970. When Long Island University student Judy Heumann was denied a teaching license because of her disability, she sued the city of New York. Through the publicity surrounding the case, Huemann found the support to start the organization. DIA would one day be the first organization to file a lawsuit under the Americans with Disabilities Act, calling for the Empire State Building in New York City to be made accessible by adding ramps.

After President Nixon vetoed the bill, legislators retooled it to satisfy Nixon's objections. In September 1973, the Rehabilitation Act finally passed. The bill brought significant change for Americans with disabilities. The new law had been written to emphasize the federal government's role in addressing social discrimination. It provided funding for the National Center for Deaf-Blind Youths and Adults. The new legislation required the federal government to comply with the 1968 Architectural Barriers Act. Importantly, the new law's Title V required the federal government's departments to hire more workers with disabilities.

One portion of the law proved highly significant—Section 504. This section was only one sentence located at the end of the new law. It had not even been a part of the original bill. The sentence read: "No otherwise qualified handicapped individual in the United States . . . shall, solely by reason of his handicap, be excluded from participation in, be denied the benefits of, or be subjected to discrimination under any program or activity receiving Federal financial assistance."[3]

FORERUNNERS TO SECTION 504

Section 504 was modeled on existing laws protecting other groups from discrimination. The Civil Rights Act of 1964 had included the groundbreaking Title VI. It stated that anyone receiving federal money could not discriminate against an individual or a group. By the early 1970s, Title VI provided the model for a new law to prohibit discrimination against women. Mirroring Title VI was Title IX of the Education Amendments of 1972. Under Title IX, schools could not discriminate against female students in education programs, including sports programs.

At the time, no one seemed certain how important Section 504 would be. Some thought it only represented a symbolic gesture. After all, it did not apply to the hiring practices of any entity but the government. Others thought it needed to be worded more specifically. Still others saw it as the most important part of the whole law. As one advocate wrote: "[Section 504] offers the one unifying key to mainstreaming of the disabled population into the general community on all fronts in a cohesive and orderly manner."[4] In addition, Section 504 cemented previous federal court decisions that public schools could not exclude children with disabilities.

FIGHTING FOR ACCESSIBILITY

Activist groups such as the DIA made significant and specific contributions to the fight for disability rights during the 1960s and 1970s. During the 1970s, the disability rights movement saw the founding of more activist organizations. One such group was the United Handicapped Federation (UHF).

The group was founded in Minneapolis and Saint Paul, Minnesota. Its organizers announced their intention to "become a strong consumer advocate for its constituents in the major areas of transportation, housing, architectural barriers and employment."[5] The UHF saw its greatest successes during the late 1970s. One of its early efforts was to consult during the construction of a 90-unit apartment complex in south Minneapolis. The complex was one of the first large-scale apartment construction projects designed for people with physical disabilities in the country.

The UHF also pursued transportation policy issues, suing the Metropolitan Transit Commission (MTC) in 1975. Even though Section 504 was already in place, the MTC was still purchasing buses that were not accessible. However, the case dragged through the courts and new,

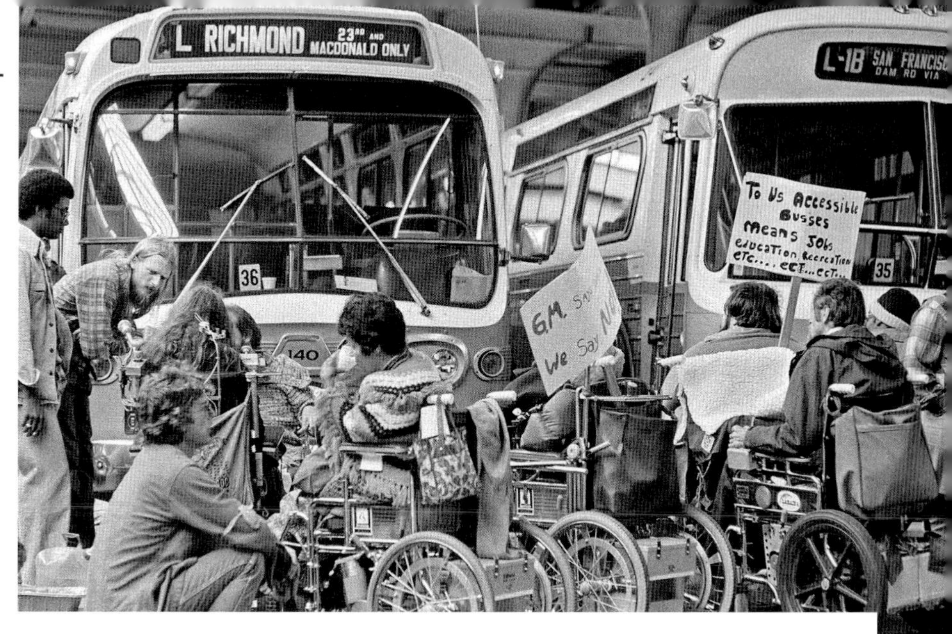

Activists protested a lack of accessible buses in San Francisco, California, in 1978.

later laws superseded the issue. By the mid-1990s, the organization disbanded, but not before its members had made significant strides for people in Minneapolis and Saint Paul with disabilities.

LEGAL LOSSES FOR PEOPLE WITH DISABILITIES

There was a perception during the 1980s that Section 504 was losing ground in the nation's courts. In 1984, the US Supreme Court made a ruling in *Grove City College v. Bell.*

As a private institution, Grove City College had avoided complying with Section 504 by refusing to accept federal and state financial funds. However, the college did enroll students who received Department of Education (DOE) grants. When a Grove City College student sued,

PROGRESS THROUGH NEW LAWS

Many acts passed by Congress after 1973 provided building blocks for the ADA law. The 1975 Developmentally Disabled Assistance and Bill of Rights Act called for a system in each state to protect the rights of people with developmental disabilities. Crucial in 1975 was the origin of the Individuals with Disabilities Education Act. This act required that children with disabilities receive a free and appropriate education in the public schools. The 1986 Protection and Advocacy for Mentally Ill Individuals Act provided funding for treatment for people with mental illnesses. That same year the Civil Rights and Remedies Equalization Act granted persons with disabilities the right to sue for violations of Section 504. Two years later, the Technology Related Assistance for Individuals with Disabilities Act increased access to assistive technologies, such as power wheelchairs and shower chairs. Also in 1988, the Fair Housing Amendments Act was passed, banning discrimination against people with disabilities purchasing or renting a home.

the DOE supported the legal challenge. The court determined there was no significant difference between the type of federal aid the college refused compared to the grants they accepted. However, the court ruled only the college's financial aid program was subject to Section 504.

This decision affected the reach of earlier laws, including Section 504, by limiting the amount of federal money that could be denied an institution for discriminating. The case had a bearing on civil rights statutes dating back to the early 1960s.

Another 1984 decision had its own

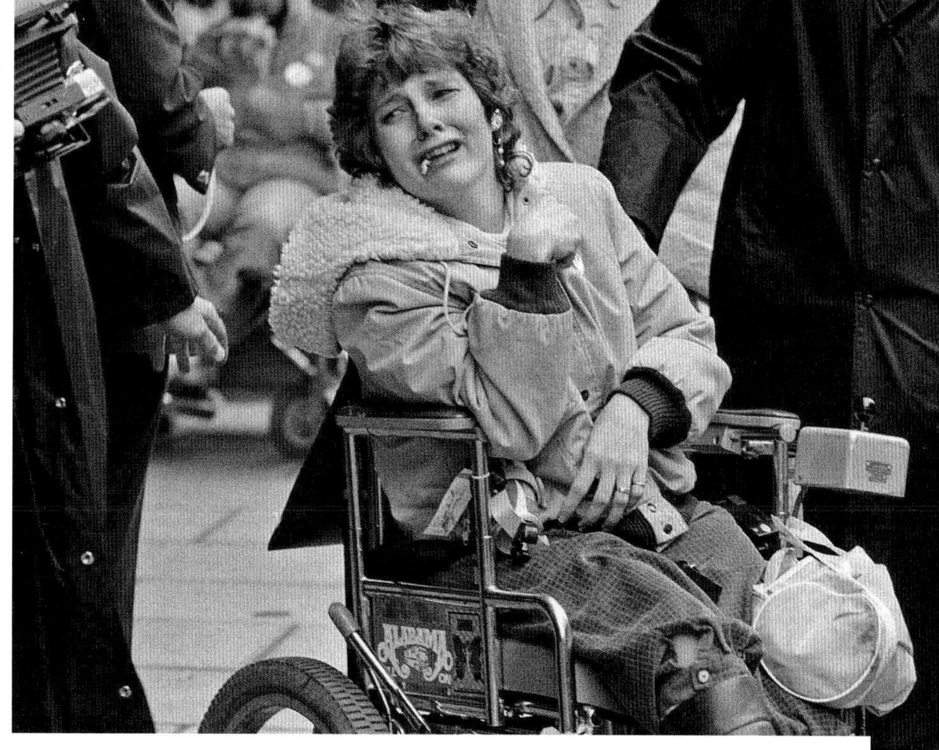

Protests for accessible facilities and program funding such as this 1984 transit protest in Washinton, DC, continued into the 1980s.

impact. In *Jacobson v. Delta Airlines*, a suit was filed because the airline required passengers with disabilities to sign a statement allowing the airline to remove them from planes at any time for unstated reasons.

Neil Jacobson, who used a wheelchair due to cerebral palsy, refused to sign the required waiver. Instead, he filed a discrimination suit against the airline. His suit argued Section 504 applied to airlines because they operated in federally regulated airports. The court did not agree, limiting the reach of existing disability laws. However, in the meantime, the government and the public were moving closer to a landmark step forward in disability rights. ●

CHAPTER 8

THE ADA: THE CAMPAIGN BEGINS

During the four decades prior to the passage of the Americans with Disabilities Act (ADA) in 1990, Congress had passed several laws in support of the rights of Americans with disabilities. Each helped establish a legal basis for what would one day be the ADA. But even combined, these earlier efforts did not accomplish together what the ADA would by itself.

« **Justin Dart Jr.,** ***left*****, would later accept the Presidential Medal of Freedom for his work for disability rights.**

Many small steps culminated in the passage of the ADA. One important element was for supporters to agree what the law itself should accomplish. In 1982, the National Council on the Handicapped, later the National Council on Disability (NCD), chose a long-standing advocate for people with disabilities to collect information to write a comprehensive policy statement, Justin Dart Jr.

Dart would become perhaps the most important voice in support of the ADA. He and Robert Burgdorf Jr. would serve on the NCD together. Despite experiencing discrimination as a young college student, Dart had been able to get a job through his wealthy father. By the 1960s, the younger Dart was working in Japan as president of Japan Tupperware.

Having achieved great personal success, Dart developed a strong sense of advocacy for people with disabilities and others who suffered discrimination. While attending the University of Houston, he had organized the school's first student club in support of racial integration on campus. At that time, minorities were barred from the university. Dart was, even then, ahead of the social curve. His club never had more than five members. Perhaps tellingly, three of the five used a wheelchair.[1]

By 1974, Dart and his wife, Yoshiko, moved to Texas. Immediately, Dart was appointed to several statewide

Seeing children with disabilities in South Vietnam solidified Dart's decision to work for disability rights.

groups in support of people with disabilities. By the early 1980s, he was appointed by the governor of Texas, William Clements, to chair the state's Task Force for Long-Range Policy for People with Disabilities. As a well-known Texas Republican, Dart was appointed to the NCD in 1981. Although his father was a close friend to President Reagan, the young Dart had gained his new appointment on his own, without any support from Justin Dart Sr.

It was a responsibility Dart had dreamed of. Once on the council, he undertook a nationwide tour traveling at his own expense. He met repeatedly with groups of people with various disabilities. Over and over, their stories rang with the same theme, one that was a reminder to Dart of his days at the University of Houston. Almost without exception, those with whom Dart spoke stated that, in addition to their disability, their lives were hampered by discrimination.

One of the first efforts made by Dart and the NCD was to compile a file of stories. Individuals with disabilities were encouraged to write to

A LIFE-CHANGING EXPERIENCE

During a visit to South Vietnam in 1967, Dart toured a facility in Saigon. In an old metal building, Dart saw Vietnamese children with polio living in terrible conditions. Dart later wrote of seeing children "with bloated bellies and matchstick arms and legs . . . their eyes bugging out, lying in their own [waste]."[2]

Witnessing the horrific treatment of children with disabilities left a deep impression. After his visit with the abandoned Vietnamese children, he met his wife, Yoshiko, in their hotel lobby and related what he had seen. He told her: "We have got to give all of our time, and energy, and passion to destroying this evil—this profound evil."[3]

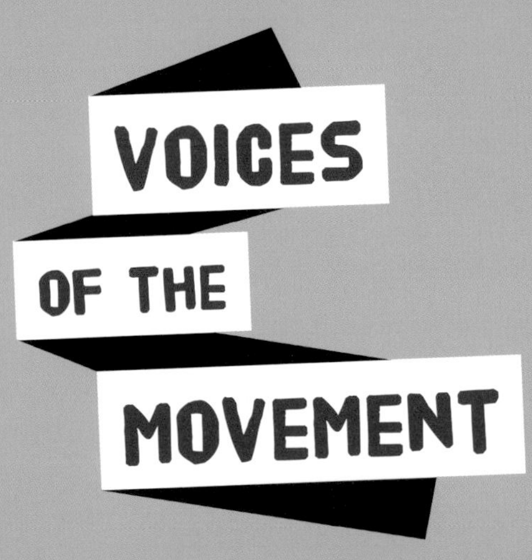

When the far-reaching Section 504 became law, some in the activist movement believed the act represented the end of the struggle for civil rights for people with disabilities. Dart did not agree. He remained committed to pursuing the next level of guarantees for the civil rights of people with disabilities. Dart wrote later:

"Around 1980 it became clear to me that we would never overcome the barriers to mainstream participation until the message of our full humanity was communicated into the consciousness and political process of America by a strong, highly visible, comprehensive civil rights law. It was equally clear that no meaningful mandate for equality could be passed or implemented until our tiny, fragmented disability community movement united, expanded, and matured in the political process."[4]

The NCD held forums to listen to the issues faced by people with disabilities around the country.

the organization and provide examples from their personal experiences of discrimination and difficulties they faced living with disabilities. Then, hearings were held across the country, where issues could be discussed and individuals with disabilities would have yet another opportunity to speak out.

TWO IMPORTANT REPORTS

In 1986 and 1988, the federal government published two reports to help the Reagan administration write legislation to support people with disabilities. The 1986 report, *Toward Independence*, was based on 1,000 telephone interviews.[5] The goal of the report was to understand the experiences and attitude of people with disabilities. It was the first time such a national survey had been done.

The report found that two of every three working-age persons with disabilities did not receive Social Security benefits or public assistance.[6] It also concluded that federal programs for people with disabilities emphasized income support too much. However, the programs did not emphasize issues such as equal opportunity and independent living enough.

The 1988 report, *On the Threshold of Independence*, was a follow-up effort to see how much progress the government had made in implementing the findings of the previous report. The report indicated that little significant progress had been made.

Then, the council wrote up a proposed policy recommending a single, new civil rights law. The council hoped the law would finally address all the discrimination issues faced by people with disabilities. In 1986, a report titled *Toward Independence* was prepared and copies were handed out to members of Congress as well as President Reagan. A second report, *On the Threshold of Independence*, was produced in 1988 and included a draft of ADA legislation. That same year, Senator Lowell Weicker of Connecticut and Representative Tony Coelho of California introduced the ADA in Congress using the version from the report.

This legislative proposal was the work of Burgdorf, the legal counsel for the NCD. He and Dart, as well as others, had hammered out the proposal together. It represented a dream to nearly everyone involved in its formation, perhaps none more than Burgdorf himself.

But the legislation went nowhere. Congress seemed disinterested, and President Reagan and his advisers appeared equally reluctant to pursue it. Despite a significant lack of support, the proposed bill did not die. In 1989, after being reworked somewhat by Bobby Silverstein, the director of the Senate Subcommittee on the Handicapped, the bill was reintroduced by Iowa senator Tom Harkin and Representative Coelho.

By this time, the Reagan administration was out of office. Vice President George H. W. Bush had been elected president in 1988. The new president was prepared to support the ADA. He had experienced disability in his own family. In 1953, Bush and his wife, Barbara, had lost their three-year-old daughter, Robin, who died of epilepsy. Two of his sons had their own disabilities: Neil had a learning disability, and Marvin's colon surgery had left him needing a device to help him go to the bathroom.

Bush had made it clear during his campaign he was a supporter of Americans with disabilities. At the

"THE HIDDEN ARMY"

President Bush was not the only government office holder who proved sympathetic to the ADA fight. Many members of Congress had their own personal stories of disability. Maryland representative Steny Hoyer's wife had epilepsy. Iowa senator Tom Harkin's brother was deaf. Massachusetts senator Edward Kennedy had a son who lost a leg to cancer. Kansas senator Bob Dole's arm was paralyzed after he was wounded in World War II. Utah senator Orrin Hatch spoke on the Senate floor about his brother-in-law who had polio.

They were all part of the "hidden army" of supporters in Congress. All along, the disabilities rights movement in US history had often made strides outside of the mainstream. The movement had often been "a largely invisible, almost underground movement."[8] With President Bush's support, the bill seemed more likely to become law.

Republican National Convention in the fall of 1988, he had stated as much: "I'm going to do whatever it takes to make sure the disabled are included in the mainstream."[7]

Activists rallied outside the US Capitol in support of the ADA. »

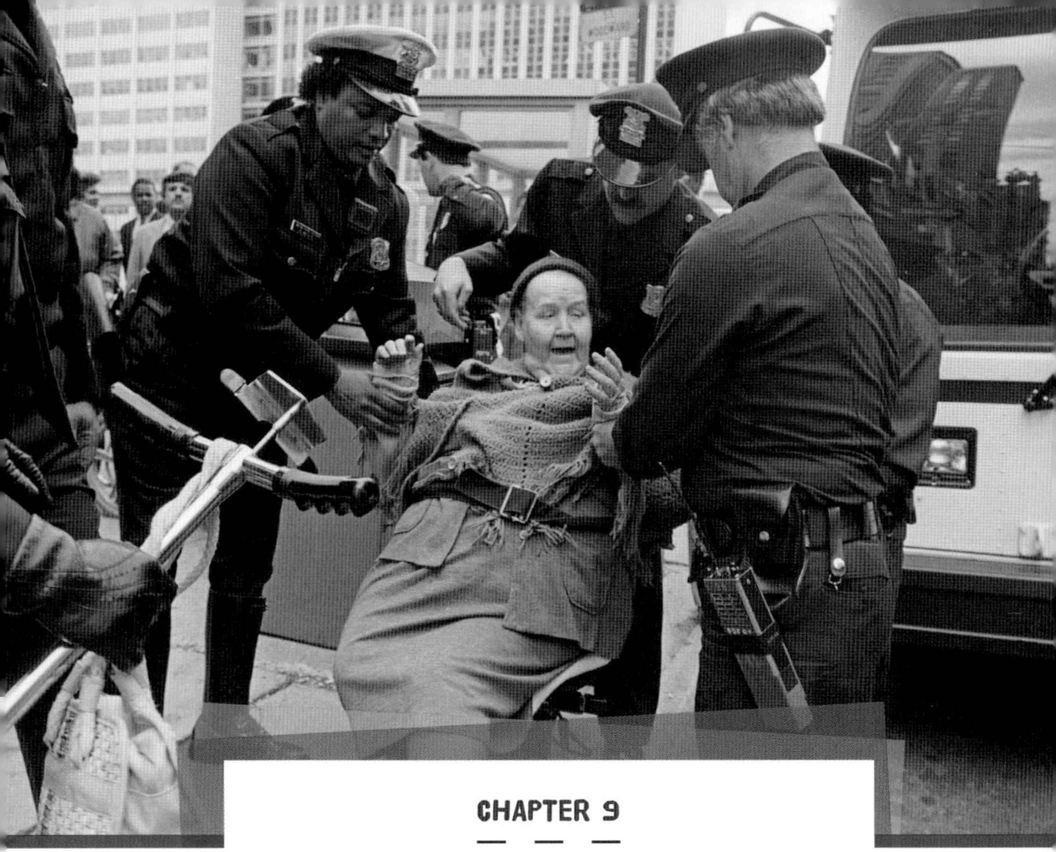

CHAPTER 9

A NEW FUTURE FOR PEOPLE WITH DISABILITIES

Tens of thousands of letters poured into the White House supporting the ADA bill. Bush sat down with influential supporters, including Evan Kemp Jr., a fellow Republican and director of the Disability Rights Center. Kemp had been appointed by Reagan in 1987 to the Equal Employment Opportunity Commission. Two years later, President Bush made him the commission's

« **Police arrest a member of the activist group American Disabled for Accessible Public Transit for blocking a bus during a protest.**

chairman. Kemp began meeting regularly with Bush's legal counsel, C. Boyden Gray, to talk about issues related to the passage of the ADA. The two men often met in Kemp's apartment for evening rounds of card games.

The proposed ADA bill was gaining momentum. Approximately 180 national organizations publicly endorsed the bill, most of which were disability-oriented groups.[1] Public demonstrations in favor of the bill were organized in Washington, DC. One was led by members of American Disabled for Accessible Public Transit (ADAPT). Its members staged a protest that included wheelchair-using activists who rallied in the US Capitol. In March 1990, nearly 500 people, many in wheelchairs, protested outside the White House in support of the ADA.[2] The group then headed off to the Capitol where Dart spoke. He had just been appointed chairman of the President's Committee on Employment of People with Disabilities. "We are Americans," he said, "and we will struggle for however long it takes for the same civil rights other Americans have."[3]

A significant wave of support for the ADA bill had finally come. Over the following months, the bill made its way through Congress. On July 26, 1990, President Bush signed the ADA bill into law. The ceremony took place on the White House lawn, where a crowd of 3,000 gathered in support.[4] Justin Dart, in his wheelchair, was seated at the president's side. Before taking up his pen, Bush said to the excited crowd:

> *I know there may have been concerns that the ADA may be vague or costly, or may lead endlessly to litigation. But I want to reassure you right now that my administration and the United States Congress have carefully crafted this Act. . . . Let the shameful wall of exclusion finally come tumbling down.*[5]

Once he had signed, the president gave Evan Kemp "an affectionate kiss on the head."[6]

One of those thousands in the crowd

ADAPT AND THE BUS FIGHT

The disability activist organization American Disabled for Accessible Public Transit (ADAPT) was only one of the important groups that pushed to pass the ADA. The group was founded in 1983. Its purpose was to organize and empower people with disabilities to participate in direct, confrontational protest. One of its early priorities was a call for public buses to be equipped with lifts for those using wheelchairs.

As one member of the organization, Mark Johnson of Atlanta, Georgia, observed: "Black people fought for the right to ride in the front of the bus. We're fighting for the right to get on the bus."[7] The organization's tactics were sometimes considered too aggressive by the rest of society. They included persons with disabilities sometimes lying down in front of buses. But the group made an impact. By the time the ADA passed, requiring chairlifts on public buses, approximately half already had them.[8]

President Bush signs the ADA as Evan Kemp, *left*, and Justin Dart, *right*, observe.

attending the Bush signing of the ADA bill into law was a 19-year-old woman with cerebral palsy—Lisa Carl—who had once been denied entrance into the movie theater in Tacoma, Washington. Lisa not only attended the exciting event in support of the civil rights of Americans with disabilities, she met President Bush, who shook her hand.

PATRISHA A. WRIGHT: "THE GENERAL"

Many people helped pass the ADA bill. One working outside the government was Patrisha A. Wright. In the fight for the ADA, she was often called "the general."

Wright began attending medical school in the 1960s. However, she developed an eye disease that eventually rendered her legally blind. She could no longer be a doctor, but her disability became her inspiration. She began working with persons with disabilities, helping individuals move from institutions to community-based living facilities.

Wright joined the ranks of the disability rights activists in 1977 when she participated in a demonstration in San Francisco. In 1979, she helped found the Disability Rights Education and Defense Fund (DREDF). In 1988, she led DREDF's campaign to place people with disabilities under the Fair Housing Amendment Act. She was instrumental in passing much of the important disability-related legislation in the 1980s and 1990s.

A BIPARTISAN EFFORT

Advocates and critics of the ADA agree on one thing—passage of the ADA remains today the most important mile post on the road to full equality for the nation's people with disabilities. No single piece of legislation was ever supported by a greater cross section of disability groups. Never had these groups worked closer together than in passing the bill into law.

From the beginning, the bill had been designed to create a law that would go further than any other in guaranteeing the civil rights of Americans with disabilities.

It proved to be a bipartisan effort down to the wire. The ADA passed in both houses of Congress, where Democrats held majorities, and was signed by a Republican president. The House vote, taken on July 12, was 377 to 28, followed by the Senate vote on July 13 of 91 to 6.[9]

EXPLAINING THE ADA

The ADA covers a wide range of issues for people with disabilities, but its main focus is on prohibiting discrimination. Protection is at its heart. The Civil Rights Act of 1964 banned discrimination based on race, religion, sex, and national origin. The ADA bars discrimination based on disability.

The act defines a "disability" as "a physical or mental impairment that substantially limits one or more of the major life activities."[10] Yet determining when any one person's specific condition can be defined as a disability must be decided on a case-by-case basis.

The ADA includes several parts. Title I prevents discrimination based on disability in job applications, hiring, promotions, and firing. Title II prohibits discrimination by local and state government. This includes school districts, city and county government, and state laws. Included is all public transportation systems regulated by the US Department of Transportation. Title II also includes state and local public housing.

Since the ADA, public transportation has become more accessible.

Title III focuses on public accommodations. The law prohibits discrimination based on disability in all such places as hotels, restaurants, stores, education buildings, parks, and transportation. Under Title III, all new buildings started after July 1992 are required to follow ADA codes of construction to accommodate people with disabilities. Most commonly, this means wheelchair ramps, wider doors, and similar changes. In preexisting buildings, the requirement to adapt for people with disabilities is based on whether the changes are "easily accomplished, without much difficulty or expense."[11] Some buildings and facilities are exempt from the ADA, including private clubs and religious-based buildings, such as churches, synagogues, and mosques. Also, historic buildings are exempt if making changes would destroy the historical integrity of the building.

CONVENTION ON THE RIGHTS OF PERSONS WITH DISABILITIES

In 2006, the United Nations adopted an international treaty protecting the rights of people with disabilities. The Convention on the Rights of Persons with Disabilities "recognize[s] the inherent dignity and worth and the equal and inalienable rights of all members of the human family."[12] It calls for an end to discrimination and also for taking down barriers that prevent individuals with disabilities from participating fully in society. Countries that sign the treaty agree to make laws that protect the rights of people with disabilities. They will provide education and support so people with disabilities can participate in society and make decisions about their own lives. Countries also agree to begin awareness campaigns to educate the public in disability issues and work to make buildings, transit, and public accommodations accessible.

Title IV focuses on telecommunications. Under the law, telecommunications companies have to provide special services for their consumers with disabilities, such as a Telecommunications Device for the Deaf (TDD).

LAWS AFTER ADA

Yet the ADA did not mark the final battle of the disability rights movement. Those in the movement always saw new issues to address. Much of the energy of the disability rights movement has continued to focus on enforcing the ADA. Also, advocates remain involved in important issues in support of people with disabilities, including employment opportunities, new technologies, housing, transportation, health care, independent living, and access to education and special programs.

In 1999, President Bill Clinton signed another important disability law. Pushed by both disability rights advocates and veterans' groups, Congress passed the Ticket to Work and Work Incentives Improvement Act. Because of the act, those on Social Security disability could claim a "ticket" to receive rehabilitation or other services of their choice, including career counseling, job placement, and ongoing employment support services. To make certain the law was fully implemented, President George W. Bush signed an executive order in 2001 instructing all federal agencies to bring the Ticket to Work Act into full swing as quickly as possible.

In 2010, on the twentieth anniversary of the passage of the ADA, President Barack Obama announced changes in the enforcement of the law. The new rules had been proposed in 2004 by President George W. Bush. They had been updated to cover recreational and city facilities. The new rules affected tens of thousands of state and local government agencies and millions of private businesses. The rules altered some standards in building codes, including doors, windows, elevators,

PRESIDENT OBAMA AND DISABILITY RIGHTS

In March 2010, Congress passed the Patient Protection and Affordable Care Act, often known as "ObamaCare." The health care reform law included changes in accessibility and nondiscrimination, home and community-based services, and other issues.

In October 2010, President Obama signed the 21st Century Communications and Video Accessibility Act (CVAA). The act updates existing laws and provides access to communications for people with disabilities.

In December 2011, President Obama's Labor Department proposed a rule change for federal contractors. The contractors would make it a priority to hire workers with disabilities to make up at least 7 percent of their workforces. The proposal was based on Section 503 of the Rehabilitation Act of 1973, which requires federal contractors to promote the employment of workers with disabilities. The new proposal represented the first time the federal government had ever tried to enforce that requirement of Section 503.

AMENDING THE ADA

In 2008, the US Congress amended the ADA in an effort to overturn four Supreme Court decisions that had narrowly interrupted the protections provided by the ADA. The new act—called the Americans with Disabilities Act Amendments Act—placed a new emphasis on defining the term *disability* as broadly as possible to maximize the extent of the ADA. Such an approach is intended to make the courts have less trouble determining when the law applies.

and bathrooms. In addition, with passage of the Affordable Health Care Act in 2010, people with disabilities could no longer be denied health-care coverage due to preexisting conditions. Signed on October 5, 2010, the symbolically important Rosa's Law removed the hurtful terms "mentally retarded" and "mental retardation" from federal laws and policies. Now, federal documents use inclusive, people-first language such as "intellectual disability" and "individual with an intellectual disability."[13]

AN ENDURING BATTLE

Since the passage of the ADA in 1990, Americans with disabilities continue to speak out on their own behalf. Over the more than 20 years since ADA passage, tens of thousands of lawsuits have been filed in the nation's courts concerning the rights of people with disabilities.

Legislation has improved the lives of people with disabilities, but protesters remain active to protect their rights and secure funding for programs.

Will the fight ever end? It is unlikely. But those with disabilities know the law is on their side. They know a long list of reforms and protections is in place in the United States, all to help support people with disabilities. People must continue to speak out. As disabilities activist Greg Solas once wrote: "Nobody should be intimidated by the law. The laws were designed for people to use. . . . We should be able to use the door of justice as well."[14] ●

TIMELINE

1636 Plymouth Colony passes law to provide support for any male with disabilities while providing military service for the colony.

1694 A Massachusetts law is passed requiring each town to provide for its citizens with mental illnesses.

1817 The American Asylum for the Deaf is founded in Hartford, Connecticut.

1841 Dorothea Dix begins her work to improve conditions for people with mental illness and intellectual disabilities, including establishing worker's compensation.

1900s–1920s The Progressive Era and World War I bring new laws and programs in support of people with disabilities.

1927 The *Buck v. Bell* Supreme Court decision rules that forced sterilization of people with disabilities is not a violation of their constitutional rights.

1935 President Franklin D. Roosevelt signs the Social Security Act on August 14.

1938 The March of Dimes campaign begins to aid polio survivors and fund polio research.

1942 Paul Strachan founds the American Federation of the Physically Handicapped, the first cross-disability national organization to battle job discrimination.

1954	The Vocational Rehabilitation Amendments are passed, funding programs for people with disabilities.
1962	Edward Roberts enters the University of California, Berkeley as the first student with disabilities.
1968	The Architectural Barriers Act prohibits architectural barriers in all federal buildings.
1970	The activist group Disabled in Action is founded.
1973	The Rehabilitation Act of 1973 is passed, including Section 504.
1986	The National Council on the Handicapped issues its first report, *Toward Independence*, outlining the legal status of Americans with disabilities.
1990	The Americans with Disabilities Act is signed into law by President George H. W. Bush on July 26.
2006	The United Nations adopts the Convention on the Rights of Persons with Disabilities, an international treaty protecting the rights of people with disabilities.
2010	Rosa's Law updates federal documents to use inclusive, people-first terminology.

ESSENTIAL FACTS

PERCENTAGE OF PEOPLE AGED 21–64 WITH A DISABILITY LIVING BELOW THE POVERTY LINE: 2011

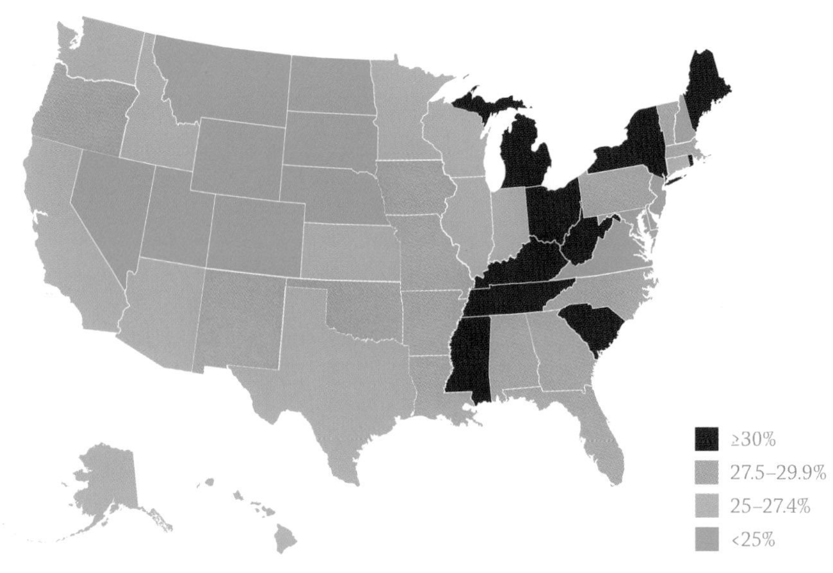

DATE OF THE MOVEMENT'S BEGINNING

The first activist groups formed in the 1930s during the Great Depression.

LOCATIONS

Washington, DC; local protests around the country

KEY PLAYERS

Disability law specialist **Robert L. Burgdorf Jr.** and activist **Justin Dart Jr.** helped write the Americans with Disabilities Act.

DISABILITY PREVALENCE BY AGE: 2010

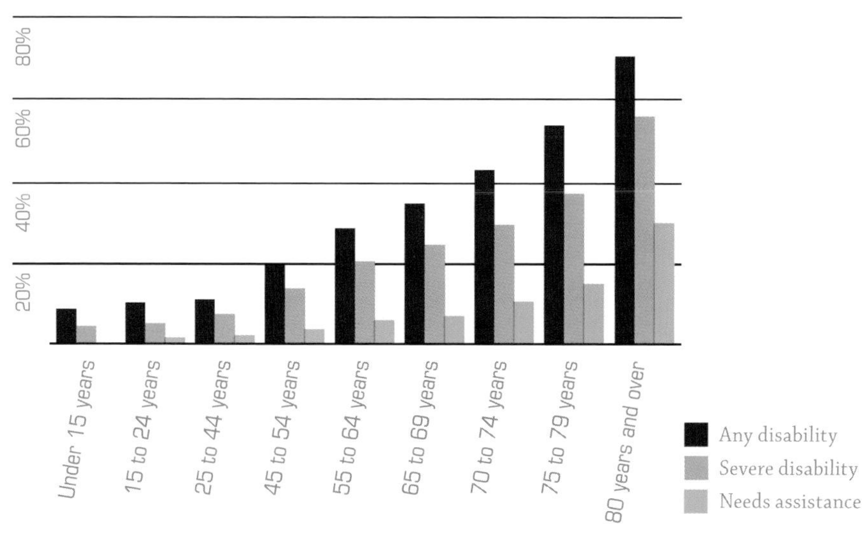

Reformer **Dorothea Dix** worked to improve institution conditions for people with mental illness.

Edward Roberts sued the University of California, Berkeley, so he could enroll. Others with disabilities soon followed.

GOALS AND OUTCOMES

People with disabilities became increasingly visible in US society after the American Civil War, World War I, and World War II. Starting in the 1960s, the independent living movement called for society to adapt for people with disabilities, rather than the other way around. Laws including the Architectural Barriers Act and the Americans with Disabilities Act mandated transportation and buildings became increasingly accessible. The movement still works to keep programs funded and protect people with disabilities.

GLOSSARY

accessible
Easy to get at, reach, or enter.

accommodation
Any adjustment in a program, facility, or policy that makes it possible for an individual with a disability to participate or benefit from it.

amputee
A person who has lost a limb or limbs.

architectural barrier
Any part of a building or structure, such as stairs or steep inclines, that makes it difficult for people with mobility impairments to gain entrance or otherwise move around.

assistive technology
Technology used to enhance the lifestyle of a person with disabilities, such as wheelchairs, leg braces, specialized computers, or other devices.

asylum
An institution that cares for the sick and for those with mental illness.

cerebral palsy
A disability resulting from damage to the brain before or after birth. Typical symptoms include bodily stiffness and rigidity or otherwise uncontrollable physical movements, including spasms or jerking.

disability
A physical or mental condition that limits the ability of someone to perform everyday tasks.

intellectual disability
A condition of the brain that limits a person's ability to learn or even understand the world around him or her. Such a condition may affect one's speech, physical movements, or other abilities.

polio
A disease that targets the body's muscular system, causing weakness or even paralysis. The disease is treatable today with a simple vaccine.

prostheses
Artificial devices that replace a missing or impaired body part.

rehabilitation
The process of providing training to an individual with a disability for the purpose of reentering the labor force.

vocational
Of or relating to training for a job or career.

welfare
Aid provided to those in need, including the unemployed, the poor, or those requiring special assistance. Such aid is typically provided by a government agency.

ADDITIONAL RESOURCES

SELECTED BIBLIOGRAPHY

Nielsen, Kim E. *A Disability History of the United States.* Boston, MA: Beacon, 2012. Print.

Pelka, Fred. *What We Have Done: An Oral History of the Disability Rights Movement.* Amherst: U of Massachusetts P, 2012. Print.

Stroman, Duane F. *The Disability Rights Movement: From Deinstitutionalization to Self-Determination.* Lanham, MY: UP of America, 2003. Print.

Switzer, Jacqueline Vaughn. *Disabled Rights: American Disability Policy and the Fight for Equality.* Washington, DC: Georgetown UP, 2003. Print.

FURTHER READINGS

Gold, Susan Dudley. *Landmark Legislation: Americans with Disabilities Act.* New York: Benchmark, 2010. Print.

Lewis, Barbara. *The Kid's Guide to Service Projects: Over 500 Service Ideas for Young People Who Want to Make a Difference.* Minneapolis, MN: Free Spirit, 2009. Print.

Muckenhoupt, Meg. *Dorothea Dix: Advocate for Mental Health Care.* New York: Oxford UP, 2003. Print.

WEB SITES

To learn more about the disability rights movement, visit ABDO Publishing Company online at **www.abdopublishing.com**. Web sites about the disability rights movement are featured on our Book Links page. These links are routinely monitored and updated to provide the most current information available.

PLACES TO VISIT

Glore Psychiatric Museum

3406 Frederick Avenue
Saint Joseph, MO 64508
1-800-530-8866
http://www.stjosephmuseum.org/glore.htm
The Glore Psychiatric Museum features exhibits tracing the institution's 130-year history as well as the evolution of mental health care in the United States.

Museum of Disability History

3826 Main Street
Buffalo, NY 14226
716-629-3626
http://museumofdisability.org
The Museum of Disability History examines the evolution of disability rights and care in the country. It includes exhibits on adaptive equipment, sports and disability, disability in pop culture, and many more topics.

SOURCE NOTES

CHAPTER 1. OVERCOMING DISABILITY

1. Joseph P. Shapiro. *No Pity: People with Disabilities Forging a New Civil Rights Movement*. New York: Times, 1993. Print. 107.
2. Ibid.
3. Ibid.
4. Ibid.
5. Ibid.
6. Kim E. Nielsen. *A Disability History of the United States*. Boston, MA: Beacon, 2012. Print. 138.
7. Joseph P. Shapiro. *No Pity: People with Disabilities Forging a New Civil Rights Movement*. New York: Times, 1993. Print. 106.
8. Ibid. 108.
9. Ibid. 105.
10. Ibid. 110.

CHAPTER 2. "LASHED INTO OBEDIENCE"

1. Kim E. Nielsen. *A Disability History of the United States*. Boston, MA: Beacon, 2012. Print. 25.
2. Ibid. 76.
3. Carol Berkin, et al. *American Voices: A History of the United States*. Glenview, IL: Scott Foresman, 1992. Print. 173.
4. "Memorial to the Massachusetts Legislature (1843), Dorothea Dix." *InfoUSA*. US Department of State, n.d. Web. 1 Apr. 2013.

CHAPTER 3. THE RISE OF DISABILITY INSTITUTIONS

1. "American Civil War." *Encyclopedia Britannica*. Encyclopedia Britannica, 2013. Web. 9 Mar. 2013.
2. Kim E. Nielsen. *A Disability History of the United States*. Boston, MA: Beacon, 2012. Print. 84.
3. "Life in Civil War America: Victories and Losses." *History E-Library: Civil War Series*. US National Park Service, 14 Mar. 2011. Web. 1 Apr. 2013.
4. Susan Schweik. *The Ugly Laws: Disability in Public*. New York: New York UP, 2009. Print. 291.
5. Ibid. 293.
6. Kim E. Nielsen. *A Disability History of the United States*. Boston, MA: Beacon, 2012. Print. 85.
7. Ibid. 96.
8. Ibid.
9. William Spratling. "An Ideal Colony for Epileptics and the Necessity for the Broader Treatment of Epilepsy." *American Medicine* 2.8 (24 Aug. 1901): 288. *Google Book Search*. Web. 1 Apr. 2013.

10. Kim E. Nielsen. *A Disability History of the United States*. Boston, MA: Beacon, 2012. Print. 103.

11. Ibid. 108.

12. William Spratling. "An Ideal Colony for Epileptics and the Necessity for the Broader Treatment of Epilepsy." *American Medicine* 2.8 (24 Aug. 1901): 287. *Google Book Search*. Web. 1 Apr. 2013.

13. Kim E. Nielsen. *A Disability History of the United States*. Boston, MA: Beacon, 2012. Print. 103.

14. Ibid. 100.

CHAPTER 4. "JOBS, NOT TIN CUPS"

1. Richard K. Scotch. *From Good Will to Civil Rights: Transforming Federal Disability Policy*. Philadelphia, PA: Temple UP, 1984. Print. 33.

2. "About Disabled American Veterans." *DAV.org*. Disabled American Veterans, 2013. Web. 3 Apr. 2013.

3. Kim E. Nielsen. *A Disability History of the United States*. Boston, MA: Beacon, 2012. Print. 129.

4. "Report of Proceedings of the First National Conference on Vocational Rehabilitation of Persons Disabled in Industry or Otherwise." *Federal Board for Vocational Education*. Government Printing Office, 1922. *Internet Archive*. Web. 3 Apr. 2013.

5. Kim E. Nielsen. *A Disability History of the United States*. Boston, MA: Beacon, 2012. Print. 132.

6. Ibid. 132–133.

7. Ibid. 134.

CHAPTER 5. POLIO, WAR, AND NEW VIEWS

1. Kim E. Nielsen. *A Disability History of the United States*. Boston, MA: Beacon, 2012. Print. 149.

2. Ibid. 148.

3. Joseph Shapiro. "WWII Pacifists Exposed Mental Ward Horrors." *NPR*. NPR, 30 Dec. 2009. Web. 3 Apr. 2013.

4. Robert S. Allen. "He Helped Handicapped." *Tuscaloosa News*, 13 Aug. 1949. *Google News*. Web. 3 Apr. 2013.

5. Ruth O'Brien. *Crippled Justice: The History of Modern Disability Policy in the Workplace*. Chicago, IL: U of Chicago P, 2001. Print. 77.

6. Kim E. Nielsen. *A Disability History of the United States*. Boston, MA: Beacon, 2012. Print. 151.

CHAPTER 6. THE INDEPENDENT LIVING MOVEMENT

1. "About Independent Living." *National Council on Independent Living*. National Council on Independent Living, 2013. Web. 3 Apr. 2013.

2. Fred Pelka. *What We Have Done: An Oral History of the Disability Rights Movement*. Amherst: U of Massachusetts P, 2012. Print. 205.

3. Eunice Kennedy Shriver. “Hope for Retarded Children.” *Saturday Evening Post* 22 Sept. 1962: 72. *Saturday Evening Post*. Web. 3 Apr. 2013.

4. Kim E. Nielsen. *A Disability History of the United States*. Boston, MA: Beacon, 2012. Print. 164.

CHAPTER 7. ACTIVISTS AND SECTION 504

1. Kim E. Nielsen. *A Disability History of the United States*. Boston, MA: Beacon, 2012. Print. 165.

2. “Disability History and Awareness Month: The Architectural Barriers Act Passes in 1968.” *Office of the Governor Rick Perry*. The State of Texas Governor, 19 Oct. 2012. Web. 3 Apr. 2013.

3. Jacqueline Vaughn Switzer. *Disabled Rights: American Disability Policy and the Fight for Equality*. Washington, DC: Georgetown UP, 2003. Print. 60.

4. Ibid.

5. Kim E. Nielsen. *A Disability History of the United States*. Boston, MA: Beacon, 2012. Print. 172.

CHAPTER 8. THE ADA: THE CAMPAIGN BEGINS

1. “Remembering Justin Dart.” *Action Online: Magazine of the United Spinal Association*. United Spinal’s Action Online, 3 July 2005. Web. 3 Apr. 2013.

2. Joseph P. Shapiro. *No Pity: People with Disabilities Forging a New Civil Rights Movement*. New York: Times, 1993. Print. 110.

3. Fred Pelka. *What We Have Done: An Oral History of the Disability Rights Movement*. Amherst: U of Massachusetts P, 2012. Print. 173.

4. Jacqueline Vaughn Switzer. *Disabled Rights: American Disability Policy and the Fight for Equality*. Washington, DC: Georgetown UP, 2003. Print. 91.

5. Peter David Blanck and David L. Braddock. *The Americans With Disabilities Act and the Emerging Workforce: Employment of People With Mental Retardation*. Washington, DC: American Association on Mental Retardation, 1998. 64. *Google Book Search*. Web. 3 Apr. 2013.

6. Ibid.

7. Joseph P. Shapiro. *No Pity: People with Disabilities Forging a New Civil Rights Movement*. New York: Times, 1993. Print. 124.

8. Ibid. 117.

CHAPTER 9. A NEW FUTURE FOR PEOPLE WITH DISABILITIES

1. Joseph P. Shapiro. *No Pity: People with Disabilities Forging a New Civil Rights Movement*. New York: Times, 1993. Print. 128.

2. Ibid. 131.

3. Ibid. 132.

4. Ibid. 140.

5. "Remarks of President George Bush at the Signing of the Americans with Disabilities Act." *EEOC.gov*. US Equal Employment Opportunity Commission, n.d. Web. 3 Apr. 2013.

6. Joseph P. Shapiro. *No Pity: People with Disabilities Forging a New Civil Rights Movement*. New York: Times, 1993. Print. 140.

7. Ibid. 128.

8. Mary Johnson and Barrett Shaw. *To Ride the Public's Buses: The Fight That Built a Movement*. Louisville, KY: Advocado, 2001. Print. 182.

9. "Testimony of Chai Feldblum to the Senate Health, Education, Labor and Pension (HELP) Committee, Hearing on Restoring Congressional Intent and Protections under the ADA (15 Nov. 2007)." *Archive ADA*. Georgetown Law, n.d. Web. 3 Apr. 2013.

10. "Disability Law Index—Disability: Definition." *ILRU.org*. Independent Living Research Utilization, n.d. Web. 3 Apr. 2013.

11. "Lesson Four: Removing Barriers in Buildings That Are Not Being Remodeled, Renovated, or Altered." *Reaching Out to Customers with Disabilities*. ADA.gov, 16 Sept. 2005. Web. 3 Apr. 2013.

12. "Convention on the Rights of Persons with Disabilities." *United Nations*. United Nations, 13 Dec. 2006. Web. 3 Apr. 2013.

13. "Rosa's Law." *Special Olympics*. Special Olympics, 23 Sept. 2012. Web. 3 Apr. 2013.

14. Barrett Shaw. *The Ragged Edge: The Disability Experience from the Pages of the First Fifteen Years of the* Disability Rag. Louisville, KY: Advocado, 1994. Print. 159.

INDEX

ABOUT THE AUTHOR

Tim McNeese is associate professor of history and department chair at York College in York, Nebraska. He has published more than 110 books and educational materials. His writing has earned him a citation in the library reference work *Contemporary Authors* and multiple citations in *Best Books for Young Teen Readers*. In 2006, Tim appeared on the History Channel program, *Risk Takers, History Makers: John Wesley Powell and the Grand Canyon*. He has been a faculty member at the Tony Hillerman Writers Conference in Albuquerque, New Mexico.

ABOUT THE CONSULTANT

William N. Myhill is an adjunct professor of law at Syracuse University and the director of legal research for the Burton Blatt Institute. He has more than 20 years of professional experience in law and education, collaborating with and providing services for diverse individuals with disabilities and cultural/linguistic differences through extensive research, teaching, and advocacy in the United States and abroad.